Ninja Foodi Smart Dual Zone
Air Fryer Cookbook for Beginners

1800 Days Healthy and Tasty Recipes for Master the Ninja Dual Zone Air Fryer

Erline L. Wilson

All Rights Reserved.

The contents of this book may not be reproduced, copied or transmitted without the direct written permission of the author or publisher. Under no circumstances will the publisher or the author be held responsible or liable for any damage, compensation or pecuniary loss arising directly or indirectly from the information contained in this book.

Legal notice. This book is protected by copyright. It is intended for personal use only. You may not modify, distribute, sell, use, quote or paraphrase any part or content of this book without the consent of the author or publisher.

Notice Of Disclaimer.

Please note that the information in this document is intended for educational and entertainment purposes only. Every effort has been made to provide accurate, up-to-date, reliable and complete information. No warranty of any kind is declared or implied. The reader acknowledges that the author does not engage in the provision of legal, financial, medical or professional advice. The content in this book has been obtained from a variety of sources. Please consult a licensed professional before attempting any of the techniques described in this book. By reading this document, the reader agrees that in no event shall the author be liable for any direct or indirect damages, including but not limited to errors, omissions or inaccuracies, resulting from the use of the information in this document.

CONTENTS

INTRODUCTION 11

BREAD AND BREAKFAST 12

    Chocolate Almond Crescent Rolls 12

    Peach Fritters 12

    Smooth Walnut-banana Loaf 13

    Filled French Toast 13

    Soft Pretzels 14

    Farmers Market Quiche 14

    Banana-strawberry Cakecups 15

    Cheesy Olive And Roasted Pepper Bread 15

    Baked Eggs 15

    Spinach-bacon Rollups 16

    Cinnamon Pumpkin Donuts 16

    Walnut Pancake 17

    Breakfast Frittata 17

    Home-style Pumpkin Crumble 17

    Easy Vanilla Muffins 18

    Sweet-hot Pepperoni Pizza 18

    Crispy Chicken Cakes 19

    Mini Everything Bagels 19

    Egg Muffins 20

    Apple-cinnamon-walnut Muffins 20

APPETIZERS AND SNACKS **21**

    Cheesy Pigs In A Blanket 21

    Rich Clam Spread 21

    Spicy Sweet Potato Tater-tots 22

    Maple Loaded Sweet Potatoes 22

    Spiced Parsnip Chips 22

    Crab Toasts 23

    Cinnamon Pita Chips 23

    Cherry Chipotle Bbq Chicken Wings 24

    Shrimp Toasts 24

    Basil Feta Crostini 25

    Beer-battered Onion Rings 25

    Roasted Tomatillo Salsa 25

    Thai-style Crab Wontons 26

    Fried Goat Cheese 26

    Mouth-watering Vegetable Casserole 27

    Sausage & Cauliflower Balls 27

    Sweet Potato Chips 28

    Jalapeño & Mozzarella Stuffed Mushrooms 28

    Thyme Sweet Potato Chips 28

    Potato Samosas 29

POULTRY RECIPES **30**

    Philly Chicken Cheesesteak Stromboli 30

    Lemon Sage Roast Chicken 30

    Crispy Duck With Cherry Sauce 31

- Hawaiian Chicken 32
- Sweet Nutty Chicken Breasts 32
- Coconut Curry Chicken With Coconut Rice 32
- Chicken Hand Pies 33
- Nacho Chicken Fries 33
- Turkey-hummus Wraps 34
- Simple Salsa Chicken Thighs 34
- Chicken Nuggets 35
- Cheesy Chicken-avocado Paninis 35
- Chicken Tenders With Basil-strawberry Glaze 35
- Saucy Chicken Thighs 36
- Basic Chicken Breasts 36
- Christmas Chicken & Roasted Grape Salad 37
- Cornish Hens With Honey-lime Glaze 37
- Fiery Chicken Meatballs 37
- Gluten-free Nutty Chicken Fingers 38
- Chicken Wings Al Ajillo 38

BEEF, PORK & LAMB RECIPES 39

- Greek Pita Pockets 39
- Beef Fajitas 39
- Honey Pork Links 40
- Tuscan Veal Chops 40
- Beef Meatballs With Herbs 41
- Asy Carnitas 41
- Kentucky-style Pork Tenderloin 41

Steak Fingers 42

T-bone Steak With Roasted Tomato, Corn And Asparagus Salsa 42

Sage Pork With Potatoes 43

Lamb Chops 43

Apple Cornbread Stuffed Pork Loin With Apple Gravy 44

Taco Pie With Meatballs 44

Crispy Lamb Shoulder Chops 45

Wiener Schnitzel 45

Beef & Barley Stuffed Bell Peppers 46

Indian Fry Bread Tacos 46

Mustard And Rosemary Pork Tenderloin With Fried Apples 47

Beef & Spinach Sautée 47

Greek-style Pork Stuffed Jalapeño Poppers 48

FISH AND SEAFOOD RECIPES 48

Lobster Tails With Lemon Garlic Butter 48

Better Fish Sticks 49

Fish Sticks With Tartar Sauce 49

Beer-battered Cod 49

Caribbean Jerk Cod Fillets 50

Fish Cakes 50

Aromatic Ahi Tuna Steaks 51

Smoked Paprika Cod Goujons 51

Crunchy Clam Strips 52

Fish Tortillas With Coleslaw 52

Basil Mushroom & Shrimp Spaghetti 52

Cilantro Sea Bass 53

Crab Cakes 53

Halibut With Coleslaw 54

Quick Tuna Tacos 54

Classic Crab Cakes 54

Fried Scallops 55

Flounder Fillets 55

Chinese Firecracker Shrimp 56

Fish Goujons With Tartar Sauce 56

VEGETARIAN RECIPES 57

Tropical Salsa 57

Rainbow Quinoa Patties 57

Sweet Corn Bread 58

Pineapple & Veggie Souvlaki 58

Cauliflower Steaks Gratin 58

Farfalle With White Sauce 59

Colorful Vegetable Medley 59

Italian-style Fried Cauliflower 60

Stuffed Portobellos 60

Egg Rolls 60

Spicy Bean Patties 61

Easy Cheese & Spinach Lasagna 61

Kale & Lentils With Crispy Onions 62

Vietnamese Gingered Tofu 62

Easy Zucchini Lasagna Roll-ups 63

- Eggplant Parmesan 63
- Crispy Apple Fries With Caramel Sauce 64
- Vegetable Couscous 64
- Tortilla Pizza Margherita 64
- Smoky Sweet Potato Fries 65

VEGETABLE SIDE DISHES RECIPES 65

- Goat Cheese Stuffed Portobellos 65
- Blistered Green Beans 66
- Hasselback Garlic-and-butter Potatoes 66
- Moroccan-spiced Carrots 67
- Garlicky Brussels Sprouts 67
- Mashed Potato Pancakes 67
- Curried Cauliflower With Cashews And Yogurt 68
- Latkes 68
- Roast Sweet Potatoes With Parmesan 69
- Stuffed Onions 69
- Buttered Brussels Sprouts 70
- Beet Fries 70
- Famous Potato Au Gratin 70
- Simple Roasted Sweet Potatoes 71
- Thyme Sweet Potato Wedges 71
- Stunning Apples & Onions 72
- Fried Corn On The Cob 72
- Herbed Baby Red Potato Hasselback 72
- Parmesan Asparagus 73

Roasted Garlic And Thyme Tomatoes 73

SANDWICHES AND BURGERS RECIPES 74

Chicken Saltimbocca Sandwiches 74

Inside-out Cheeseburgers 74

Thanksgiving Turkey Sandwiches 75

Black Bean Veggie Burgers 75

Asian Glazed Meatballs 76

Chicken Club Sandwiches 77

Thai-style Pork Sliders 77

Chicken Spiedies 78

Sausage And Pepper Heros 78

Crunchy Falafel Balls 79

Salmon Burgers 79

Dijon Thyme Burgers 80

Inside Out Cheeseburgers 80

Eggplant Parmesan Subs 81

Chili Cheese Dogs 81

Reuben Sandwiches 82

Chicken Apple Brie Melt 82

Best-ever Roast Beef Sandwiches 83

Perfect Burgers 83

Philly Cheesesteak Sandwiches 84

DESSERTS AND SWEETS 85

Dark Chocolate Cream Galette 85

Blueberry Crisp 85

Spanish Churro Bites 86

Fruity Oatmeal Crisp 86

Nutty Cookies 86

Cinnamon Canned Biscuit Donuts 87

Orange Gooey Butter Cake 87

Cherry Hand Pies 88

Cheesecake Wontons 88

Fruit Turnovers 89

Midnight Nutella® Banana Sandwich 89

Giant Vegan Chocolate Chip Cookie 89

Donut Holes 90

S'mores Pockets 90

Guilty Chocolate Cookies 91

Carrot-oat Cake Muffins 91

Custard 92

Chocolate Soufflés 92

Chocolate Macaroons 93

Peanut Butter S'mores 93

INDEX 94

INTRODUCTION

Are you tired of the monotony of fried meals? Do you own an air fryer but haven't explored its full potential? Are you seeking healthier, low-fat, and nutritious alternatives for your family's meals?

If you answered yes to any of these questions, then our collection of recipes is perfect for you. Say goodbye to greasy, calorie-laden dishes and hello to flavorful, guilt-free meals that are quick and easy to prepare.

The benefits of our Ninja Air Fryer Recipe Book for beginners and advanced users are numerous:

Achieve crispy dishes with minimal oil, keeping them low in fat and carbs.
Explore a variety of nutritious and flavorful recipes, including poultry, seafood, and desserts.
Follow our easy-to-understand, step-by-step instructions and cooking times, suitable for all skill levels.
Simplify your shopping with organized lists and affordable ingredients, reducing clutter in your pantry.
Enjoy unsupervised cooking experiences in 30 minutes or less, perfect for busy weeknights.

Indulge in a Culinary Adventure:
Vibrant vegetarian and vegan creations
Savory seafood sensations
Mouthwatering appetizers
Tender poultry, succulent pork, and juicy beef dishes
Comforting soups and salads bursting with flavor
Decadent desserts to satisfy your sweet tooth
 ....and much more

Get a copy of this amazing Air Fryer Cookbook now and start cooking your delicious meals today!

Bread And Breakfast

Chocolate Almond Crescent Rolls

Servings: 4 | Prep Time: 10 Minutes | Cooking Time: 8 Minutes

Ingredients:

- 1 (225 g) tube of crescent roll dough
- 170 g semi-sweet or bittersweet chocolate chunks
- 1 egg white, lightly beaten
- ¼ cup sliced almonds
- Powdered sugar, for dusting
- Butter or oil

Directions:

1. Preheat the air fryer to 180°C/350°F.
2. Unwrap the crescent roll dough and separate it into triangles with the points facing away from you. Place a row of chocolate chunks along the bottom edge of the dough. (If you are using chips, make it a double row.) Roll the dough up around the chocolate and then place another row of chunks on the dough. Roll again and finish with one or two chocolate chunks. Be sure to leave the end free of chocolate so that it can adhere to the rest of the roll.
3. Brush the tops of the crescent rolls with the lightly beaten egg white and sprinkle the almonds on top, pressing them into the crescent dough so they adhere.
4. Brush the bottom of the air fryer basket with butter or oil and transfer the crescent rolls to the basket. Air-fry at 180°C/350°F for 8 minutes.
5. Remove and let the crescent rolls cool before dusting with powdered sugar and serving.

Variations & Ingredients Tips:

- Use different types of chocolate, such as milk chocolate or white chocolate, for a variety of flavors.
- Add some cinnamon or nutmeg to the crescent dough for a spiced twist.
- Serve the crescent rolls with a side of fresh berries or whipped cream for a decadent breakfast or dessert.

Per Serving: Calories: 400; Total Fat: 24g; Saturated Fat: 10g; Cholesterol: 0mg; Sodium: 330mg; Total Carbs: 42g; Fiber: 3g; Sugars: 20g; Protein: 7g

Peach Fritters

Servings: 8 | Prep Time: 30 Minutes | Cooking Time: 6 Minutes

Ingredients:

- 1½ cups bread flour
- 1 tsp active dry yeast
- ¼ cup sugar
- ¼ tsp salt
- ½ cup warm milk
- ½ tsp vanilla extract
- 2 egg yolks
- 2 tbsp melted butter
- 2 cups small diced peaches (fresh or frozen)
- 1 tbsp butter
- 1 tsp ground cinnamon
- 1 to 2 tbsp sugar
- Glaze
- ¾ cup powdered sugar
- 4 tsp milk

Directions:

1. Combine the flour, yeast, sugar and salt in a bowl. Add the milk, vanilla, egg yolks and melted butter and combine until the dough starts to come together.
2. Transfer the dough to a floured surface and knead it by hand for 2 minutes. Shape into a ball, place in a large oiled bowl, cover and let rise for 1 to 1½ hours.
3. Melt 1 tbsp butter in a saucepan. Add peaches, cinnamon and sugar. Cook for 5 minutes until softened. Set aside to cool.
4. When dough has risen, shape into a 30-cm circle. Spread peaches over half and fold other half over. Score in a diamond pattern cutting through top layer only.
5. Roll up from one end into an 20-cm log. Cut into 8 slices and place on floured sheet. Let rise 30 minutes.
6. Preheat air fryer to 190°C/370°F.

7. Air-fry 2-3 fritters at a time for 3 minutes. Flip and fry 2-3 minutes more until golden.
8. Make glaze by whisking powdered sugar and milk. Let fritters cool 10 minutes then glaze.

Variations & Ingredients Tips:

- Use other fruit like apples or berries instead of peaches.
- Add spices like cinnamon or nutmeg to the dough.
- Drizzle with a vanilla glaze instead.

Per Serving: Calories: 280; Total Fat: 7g; Saturated Fat: 3.6g; Cholesterol: 75mg; Sodium: 145mg; Total Carbohydrates: 48g; Dietary Fiber: 2g; Total Sugars: 18g; Protein: 5g

Smooth Walnut-banana Loaf

Servings: 4 | Prep Time: 15 Minutes | Cooking Time: 40 Minutes

Ingredients:

- 1/3 cup peanut butter, melted
- 2 tbsp butter, melted and cooled
- ¾ cup flour
- ½ tsp salt
- ¼ tsp baking soda
- 2 ripe bananas
- 2 eggs
- 1 tsp lemon juice
- ½ cup evaporated cane sugar
- ½ cup ground walnuts
- 1 tbsp blackstrap molasses
- 1 tsp vanilla extract

Directions:

1. Preheat air fryer to 155°C/310°F.
2. Mix flour, salt, baking soda in one bowl.
3. In another bowl, mash bananas and eggs.
4. Stir in sugar, peanut butter, lemon, butter, walnuts, molasses and vanilla.
5. Fold in flour mixture just until combined.
6. Transfer to a parchment-lined baking dish.
7. Bake for 30-35 mins until a toothpick inserted in center comes out clean.

Variations & Ingredients Tips:

- Use almond or cashew butter instead of peanut.
- Add chocolate chips, coconut or chopped dates to the batter.
- Substitute some of the flour with oat or almond flour.

Per Serving: Calories: 535; Total Fat: 27g; Saturated Fat: 8g; Cholesterol: 103mg; Sodium: 489mg; Total Carbs: 66g; Dietary Fiber: 4g; Total Sugars: 39g; Protein: 12g

Filled French Toast

Servings: 4 | Prep Time: 15 Minutes | Cooking Time: 25 Minutes

Ingredients:

- 4 French bread slices
- 2 tablespoons blueberry jam
- 1/3 cup fresh blueberries
- 2 egg yolks
- 79 ml milk
- 1 tablespoon sugar
- ½ teaspoon vanilla extract
- 3 tablespoons sour cream

Directions:

1. Preheat the air fryer to 190°C/370°F. Cut a pocket into the side of each slice of bread. Don't cut all the way through. Combine the blueberry jam and blueberries and crush the blueberries into the jam with a fork. In a separate bowl, beat the egg yolks with milk, sugar, and vanilla until well combined. Smear some sour cream in the pocket of each bread slice and add the blueberry mix on top. Squeeze the edges of the bread to close the opening. Dip the bread in the egg mixture, soak for 3 minutes per side. In a single layer, put the bread in the greased frying basket and Air Fry for 5 minutes. Flip the bread and cook for 3-6 more minutes or until golden.

Variations & Ingredients Tips:

- Use strawberry, raspberry or apricot jam for different flavors.
- Stuff with cream cheese, mascarpone or ricotta mixed with sugar and cinnamon.
- Top with maple syrup, whipped cream and a dusting of powdered sugar.

Per Serving: Calories: 263; Total Fat: 9g; Saturated Fat: 4g; Cholesterol: 111mg; Sodium: 323mg; Total Carbs: 38g; Dietary Fiber: 2g; Total Sugars: 14g; Protein: 8g

Soft Pretzels

Servings: 12 | Prep Time: 20 Minutes | Cooking Time: 6 Minutes

Ingredients:

- 2 teaspoons yeast
- 1 cup water, warm
- 1 teaspoon sugar
- 1 teaspoon salt
- 2½ cups all-purpose flour
- 2 tablespoons butter, melted
- 1 cup boiling water
- 1 tablespoon baking soda
- coarse sea salt
- melted butter

Directions:

1. Combine yeast and warm water in a small bowl.
2. In mixer bowl, mix sugar, salt and flour. With mixer running, add yeast mix and melted butter. Knead 10 mins.
3. Shape into a ball, let rise 1 hour.
4. Punch down dough and divide into 12-48 pieces depending on desired pretzel size.
5. Roll each into a rope and shape into pretzel/knot.
6. Combine boiling water and baking soda in a bowl. Let cool slightly.
7. Working in batches, dip pretzels in baking soda water for 30-60 secs then place on parchment. Sprinkle with salt.
8. Preheat air fryer to 175°C/350°F. Air fry in batches for 3 mins per side.
9. Brush pretzels with melted butter when done.

Variations & Ingredients Tips:

- Add cheese, herbs or spices to the dough before shaping.
- Substitute some of the all-purpose flour with whole wheat.
- Serve with mustard, cheese sauce or other dipping sauces.

Per Serving: Calories: 118; Total Fat: 2g; Saturated Fat: 1g; Cholesterol: 5mg; Sodium: 706mg; Total Carbs: 21g; Dietary Fiber: 1g; Total Sugars: 0g; Protein: 3g

Farmers Market Quiche

Servings: 4 | Prep Time: 15 Minutes | Cooking Time: 35 Minutes

Ingredients:

- 4 button mushrooms
- ¼ medium red bell pepper
- 1 teaspoon extra-virgin olive oil
- One 23 cm pie crust, at room temperature
- ¼ cup grated carrot
- ¼ cup chopped, fresh baby spinach leaves
- 3 eggs, whisked
- 59 ml half-and-half
- ½ teaspoon thyme
- ½ teaspoon sea salt
- 57 g crumbled goat cheese or feta

Directions:

1. In a medium bowl, toss the mushrooms and bell pepper with extra-virgin olive oil; place into the air fryer basket. Set the temperature to 200°C/400°F for 8 minutes, stirring after 4 minutes. Remove from the air fryer, and roughly chop the mushrooms and bell peppers. Wipe the air fryer clean. | Prep an 18 cm oven-safe baking dish by spraying the bottom of the pan with cooking spray.
2. Place the pie crust into the baking dish; fold over and crimp the edges or use a fork to press to give the edges some shape.
3. In a medium bowl, mix together the mushrooms, bell peppers, carrots, spinach, and eggs. Stir in the half-and-half, thyme, and salt.
4. Pour the quiche mixture into the base of the pie shell. Top with crumbled cheese.
5. Place the quiche into the air fryer basket. Set the temperature to 165°C/325°F for 30 minutes.
6. When complete, turn the quiche halfway and cook an additional 5 minutes. Allow the quiche to rest 20 minutes prior to slicing and serving.

Variations & Ingredients Tips:

- Use asparagus, zucchini or broccoli instead of mushrooms and peppers.
- Add some cooked bacon, ham or sausage for a meaty version.
- Sprinkle with chopped fresh herbs like parsley or chives before serving.

Per Serving: Calories: 315; Total Fat: 21g; Saturated Fat: 9g; Cholesterol: 158mg; Sodium: 517mg; Total Carbs: 21g; Dietary Fiber: 1g; Total Sugars: 3g; Protein: 11g

Banana-strawberry Cakecups

Servings: 6 | Prep Time: 10 Minutes | Cooking Time: 25 Minutes

Ingredients:

- ½ cup mashed bananas
- ¼ cup maple syrup
- ½ cup Greek yogurt
- 1 tsp vanilla extract
- 1 egg
- 1 ½ cups all-purpose flour
- 1 tbsp cornstarch
- ½ tsp baking soda
- ½ tsp baking powder
- ½ tsp salt
- ½ cup strawberries, sliced

Directions:

1. Preheat air fryer to 182°C/360°F.
2. In a large bowl, mix mashed bananas, syrup, yogurt, vanilla and egg until smooth.
3. Sift in flour, baking soda, baking powder and salt. Stir to combine.
4. Toss strawberries with cornstarch in a small bowl, then fold into batter.
5. Divide batter evenly between greased muffin cups and place in air fryer basket.
6. Bake 12-15 minutes until golden brown and a toothpick inserted comes out clean.
7. Cool 5 minutes before serving.

Variations & Ingredients Tips:

- Use different fruit like blueberries or raspberries.
- Add chopped nuts or chocolate chips to the batter.
- Drizzle with a glaze or dust with powdered sugar when cooled.

Per Serving: Calories: 190; Total Fat: 2g; Saturated Fat: 0g; Cholesterol: 25mg; Sodium: 310mg; Total Carbs: 39g; Dietary Fiber: 2g; Total Sugars: 15g; Protein: 4g

Cheesy Olive And Roasted Pepper Bread

Servings: 8 | Prep Time: 10 Minutes | Cooking Time: 7 Minutes

Ingredients:

- 18-cm round bread boule
- Olive oil
- ½ cup mayonnaise
- 2 tablespoons butter, melted
- 1 cup grated mozzarella or Fontina cheese
- ¼ cup grated Parmesan cheese
- ½ teaspoon dried oregano
- ½ cup black olives, sliced
- ½ cup green olives, sliced
- ½ cup coarsely chopped roasted red peppers
- 2 tablespoons minced red onion
- Freshly ground black pepper

Directions:

1. Preheat air fryer to 188°C/370°F.
2. Cut bread boule in half horizontally. Trim top if rounded so halves lie flat.
3. Brush both halves lightly with olive oil.
4. Place one half cut-side down in air fryer basket. Toast at 188°C/370°F for 2 mins. Repeat with other half.
5. Mix mayonnaise, melted butter, cheeses, oregano, olives, peppers and onion. Season with black pepper.
6. Spread cheese mixture over untoasted side of bread halves.
7. Air fry at 177°C/350°F for 5 mins until cheese melts and browns. Repeat with second half.
8. Cut into slices and serve warm.

Variations & Ingredients Tips:

- Use sun-dried tomatoes or artichoke hearts instead of peppers.
- Add chopped garlic, spinach or basil to the cheese mixture.
- Brush bread with garlic butter or pesto before toasting.

Per Serving: Calories: 360; Total Fat: 27g; Saturated Fat: 8g; Cholesterol: 35mg; Sodium: 790mg; Total Carbs: 22g; Dietary Fiber: 2g; Total Sugars: 2g; Protein: 10g

Baked Eggs

Servings: 4 | Prep Time: 5 Minutes | Cooking Time: 6 Minutes

Ingredients:

- 4 large eggs
- ⅛ teaspoon black pepper
- ⅛ teaspoon salt

Directions:

1. Preheat the air fryer to 165°C/330°F. Place 4 silicone muffin liners into the air fryer basket.
2. Crack 1 egg at a time into each silicone muffin liner. Sprinkle with black pepper and salt.
3. Bake for 6 minutes. Remove and let cool 2 minutes prior to serving.

Variations & Ingredients Tips:

- Add shredded cheese, chopped herbs or cooked meats on top of eggs before baking.
- Use ramekins or oven-safe bowls instead of silicone liners.

Per Serving: Calories: 70; Total Fat: 5g; Saturated Fat: 1.5g; Cholesterol: 185mg; Sodium: 115mg; Total Carbs: 0g; Dietary Fiber: 0g; Total Sugars: 0g; Protein: 6g

Spinach-bacon Rollups

Servings: 4 | Prep Time: 10 Minutes | Cooking Time: 9 Minutes

Ingredients:

- 4 flour tortillas (15-18cm size)
- 4 slices Swiss cheese
- 1 cup baby spinach leaves
- 4 slices turkey bacon

Directions:

1. Preheat air fryer to 200°C/390°F.
2. On each tortilla, place one slice cheese, ¼ cup spinach.
3. Roll up tortillas and wrap each with a bacon slice, securing ends with toothpicks.
4. Place rollups spaced apart in air fryer basket.
5. Cook 4 mins, turn and rearrange, cook 5 more mins until bacon is crisp.

Variations & Ingredients Tips:

- Use different cheese varieties like cheddar or pepper jack.
- Add diced tomatoes, olives or roasted red peppers.
- Brush with beaten egg before cooking for a crispier crust.

Per Serving: Calories: 252; Total Fat: 13g; Saturated Fat: 5g; Cholesterol: 36mg; Sodium: 677mg; Total Carbs: 20g; Dietary Fiber: 1g; Total Sugars: 1g; Protein: 13g

Cinnamon Pumpkin Donuts

Servings: 6 | Prep Time: 20 Minutes | Cooking Time: 30 Minutes

Ingredients:

- ⅓ cup canned pumpkin purée
- 1 cup flour
- 3 tablespoons brown sugar
- ½ teaspoon ground cinnamon
- ⅛ teaspoon ground nutmeg
- 1 teaspoon baking powder
- 3 tablespoons milk
- 2 tablespoons butter, melted
- 1 large egg
- 3 tablespoons powdered sugar

Directions:

1. Combine the flour, brown sugar, cinnamon, nutmeg, and baking powder in a bowl.
2. Whisk the pumpkin, milk, butter, and egg white in another bowl.
3. Pour the pumpkin mixture over the dry ingredients and stir. Add more milk or flour if necessary to make a soft dough.
4. Cover your hands in flour, make 12 pieces from the dough, and form them into balls.
5. Measure the frying basket, then cut foil or parchment paper about 2.5 cm smaller than the measurement. Poke holes in it and put it in the basket.
6. Preheat air fryer to 180°C/360°F. Set the donut holes in the basket and Air Fry for 5-7 minutes.
7. Allow the donuts to chill for 5 minutes, then roll in powdered sugar. Serve.

Variations & Ingredients Tips:

- Use different types of winter squash, such as butternut or acorn squash, for a variety of flavors.
- Add some grated orange or lemon zest to the dough for extra flavor.
- For a chocolate version, add some cocoa powder to the dough and glaze the donuts with chocolate ganache.

Per Serving: Calories: 180; Total Fat: 6g; Saturated Fat: 3.5g; Cholesterol: 40mg; Sodium: 160mg; Total Carbs: 28g; Fiber: 1g; Sugars: 13g; Protein: 3g

Walnut Pancake

Servings: 4 | Prep Time: 10 Minutes | Cooking Time: 20 Minutes

Ingredients:

- 3 tablespoons butter, divided into thirds
- 1 cup flour
- 1½ teaspoons baking powder
- ¼ teaspoon salt
- 2 tablespoons sugar
- ¾ cup milk
- 1 egg, beaten
- 1 teaspoon pure vanilla extract
- ½ cup walnuts, roughly chopped
- maple syrup or fresh sliced fruit, for serving

Directions:

1. Place 1 tablespoon of the butter in air fryer baking pan. Cook at 165°C/330°F for 3 minutes to melt.
2. In a small dish or pan, melt the remaining 2 tablespoons of butter either in the microwave or on the stove.
3. In a medium bowl, stir together the flour, baking powder, salt, and sugar. Add milk, beaten egg, the 2 tablespoons of melted butter, and vanilla. Stir until combined but do not beat. Batter may be slightly lumpy.
4. Pour batter over the melted butter in air fryer baking pan. Sprinkle nuts evenly over top.
5. Cook for 20minutes or until toothpick inserted in center comes out clean. Turn air fryer off, close the machine, and let pancake rest for 2minutes.
6. Remove pancake from pan, slice, and serve with syrup or fresh fruit.

Variations & Ingredients Tips:

- Substitute different nuts like pecans or almonds for the walnuts.
- Add chocolate chips, berries or banana slices to the batter.
- Top with powdered sugar or whipped cream instead of syrup.

Per Serving: Calories: 300; Total Fat: 17g; Saturated Fat: 6g; Cholesterol: 60mg; Sodium: 290mg; Total Carbs: 32g; Dietary Fiber: 2g; Total Sugars: 8g; Protein: 7g

Breakfast Frittata

Servings: 2 | Prep Time: 10 Minutes | Cooking Time: 25 Minutes

Ingredients:

- 4 cooked pancetta slices, chopped
- 5 eggs
- Salt and pepper to taste
- ½ leek, thinly sliced
- ½ cup grated cheddar cheese
- 1 tomato, sliced
- 1 cup iceberg lettuce, torn
- 2 tbsp milk

Directions:

1. Preheat air fryer to 160°C/320°F.
2. Beat the eggs, milk, salt, and pepper in a bowl. Mix in pancetta and cheddar.
3. Transfer to a greased baking pan. Top with tomato slices and leek.
4. Place pan in air fryer basket and bake for 14 minutes.
5. Let cool for 5 minutes. Serve with lettuce.

Variations & Ingredients Tips:

- Add sauteed mushrooms, onions or bell peppers.
- Use different cheeses like feta or goat cheese.
- Serve with avocado slices or salsa on the side.

Per Serving: Calories: 335; Total Fat: 22g; Saturated Fat: 10g; Cholesterol: 405mg; Sodium: 610mg; Total Carbs: 10g; Dietary Fiber: 1g; Total Sugars: 4g; Protein: 23g

Home-style Pumpkin Crumble

Servings: 6 | Prep Time: 15 Minutes | Cooking Time: 60 Minutes + Chilling Time

Ingredients:

- 177 g canned pumpkin puree
- 60 g whole-wheat flour
- 63 g sugar
- ¼ teaspoon baking soda
- ¼ teaspoon baking powder
- 1 teaspoon pumpkin pie spice
- ⅛ teaspoon ground cinnamon
- ⅛ teaspoon ground nutmeg
- ⅛ teaspoon salt
- 1 tablespoon orange zest
- 14 g butter, melted
- 1 egg
- ¾ teaspoon vanilla extract
- 27 g light brown sugar

- 8 g cornflour
- ⅛ teaspoon ground cinnamon
- 8 g cold butter

Directions:

1. Combine all dry ingredients in a bowl with a whisk. In a large bowl, combine pumpkin puree, butter, egg, and vanilla. Beat these ingredients in a mixer at medium speed until thick. Slowly add 1/3 cup of the flour mixture to the pumpkin mixture at a low speed until it is combined. Pour batter into a greased baking dish. | Prepare the crumb topping by combining brown sugar, cornflour, and cinnamon in a small bowl. Using a fork, cut in the cold butter until the mixture is coarse and crumbly. Sprinkle over the batter evenly.
2. Preheat air fryer to 150°C/300°F. Put the pan in the frying basket. Bake until a toothpick in the center comes out clean, 40-45 minutes. Allow to cool for 30 minutes before cutting and serving.

Variations & Ingredients Tips:

- Use sweet potato puree or mashed bananas instead of pumpkin.
- Add some chopped pecans or walnuts to the crumble topping.
- Serve warm with a scoop of vanilla ice cream or whipped cream.

Per Serving: Calories: 185; Total Fat: 5g; Saturated Fat: 3g; Cholesterol: 36mg; Sodium: 165mg; Total Carbs: 34g; Dietary Fiber: 2g; Total Sugars: 23g; Protein: 3g

Easy Vanilla Muffins

Servings: 6 | Prep Time: 10 Minutes | Cooking Time: 35 Minutes + Cooling Time

Ingredients:

- 180 g flour
- 5 tablespoons butter, melted
- ¼ cup brown sugar
- 2 tablespoons raisins
- ½ teaspoon ground cinnamon
- ⅓ cup granulated sugar
- ¼ cup milk
- 1 large egg
- 1 teaspoon vanilla extract
- 1 teaspoon baking powder
- Pinch of salt

Directions:

1. Preheat the air fryer to 165°C/330°F.
2. Combine 45 g of flour, 2½ tablespoons of butter, brown sugar, and cinnamon in a bowl and mix until crumbly. Set aside.
3. In another bowl, combine the remaining butter, granulated sugar, milk, egg, and vanilla and stir well. Add the remaining flour, baking powder, raisins, and salt and stir until combined.
4. Spray 6 silicone muffin cups with baking spray and spoon half the batter into them. Add a teaspoon of the cinnamon mixture, then add the rest of the batter and sprinkle with the remaining cinnamon mixture, pressing into the batter.
5. Put the muffin cups in the frying basket and Bake for 14-18 minutes or until a toothpick inserted into the center comes out clean.
6. Cool for 10 minutes, then remove the muffins from the cups. Serve and enjoy!

Variations & Ingredients Tips:

- Use different types of dried fruit, such as cranberries or apricots, for a variety of flavors.
- Add some chopped nuts, such as walnuts or pecans, to the batter for extra texture.
- For a chocolate version, replace ¼ cup of flour with cocoa powder and add some chocolate chips to the batter.

Per Serving: Calories: 270; Total Fat: 12g; Saturated Fat: 7g; Cholesterol: 55mg; Sodium: 200mg; Total Carbs: 38g; Fiber: 1g; Sugars: 22g; Protein: 4g

Sweet-hot Pepperoni Pizza

Servings: 2 | Prep Time: 8 Minutes | Cooking Time: 18 Minutes

Ingredients:

- 1 (170-225g) pizza dough ball*
- Olive oil
- 1/2 cup pizza sauce
- 3/4 cup grated mozzarella cheese
- 1/2 cup thick sliced pepperoni
- 1/3 cup sliced pickled hot banana peppers
- 1/4 teaspoon dried oregano
- 2 teaspoons honey

Directions:

1. Preheat air fryer to 200°C/390°F.
2. Cut out a piece of aluminum foil the same size as the bottom of the air fryer basket. Brush the foil circle with

olive oil. Shape the dough into a circle and place it on top of the foil. Dock the dough by piercing it several times with a fork. Brush the dough lightly with olive oil and transfer it into the air fryer basket with the foil on the bottom.
3. Air-fry the plain pizza dough for 6 minutes. Turn the dough over, remove the aluminum foil and brush again with olive oil. Air-fry for an additional 4 minutes.
4. Spread the pizza sauce on top of the dough and sprinkle the mozzarella cheese over the sauce. Top with the pepperoni, pepper slices and dried oregano. Lower the temperature of the air fryer to 175°C/350°F and cook for 8 minutes, until the cheese has melted and lightly browned. Transfer the pizza to a cutting board and drizzle with the honey. Slice and serve.

Variations & Ingredients Tips:

- Use store-bought or homemade dough.
- Add other toppings like mushrooms, onions, olives.
- Sprinkle with parmesan or red pepper flakes before baking.

Per Serving: Calories: 570; Total Fat: 28g; Saturated Fat: 10g; Cholesterol: 55mg; Sodium: 1310mg; Total Carbs: 57g; Dietary Fiber: 3g; Total Sugars: 9g; Protein: 22g

Crispy Chicken Cakes

Servings: 4 | Prep Time: 10 Minutes | Cooking Time: 30 Minutes

Ingredients:

- 1 peeled Granny Smith apple, chopped
- 2 scallions, chopped
- 3 tablespoons ground almonds
- 1 teaspoon garlic powder
- 1 egg white
- 2 tablespoons apple juice
- Black pepper to taste
- 450 g ground chicken

Directions:

1. Preheat air fryer to 165°C/330°F.
2. Combine the apple, scallions, almonds, garlic powder, egg white, apple juice, and pepper in a bowl. Add the ground chicken using your hands. Mix well.
3. Make 8 patties and set four in the frying basket. Air Fry for 8-12 minutes until crispy. Repeat with the remaining patties.
4. Serve hot.

Variations & Ingredients Tips:

- Use different types of ground meat, such as turkey or pork, for a variety of flavors.
- Add some grated Parmesan cheese or bread crumbs to the patty mixture for extra flavor and texture.
- Serve the chicken cakes with a side of salsa or tzatziki sauce for dipping.

Per Serving: Calories: 240; Total Fat: 14g; Saturated Fat: 3.5g; Cholesterol: 115mg; Sodium: 120mg; Total Carbs: 6g; Fiber: 1g; Sugars: 4g; Protein: 26g

Mini Everything Bagels

Servings: 4 | Prep Time: 15 Minutes | Cooking Time: 6 Minutes

Ingredients:

- 1 cup all-purpose flour
- 2 teaspoons baking powder
- ½ teaspoon salt
- 1 cup plain Greek yogurt
- 1 egg, whisked
- 1 teaspoon sesame seeds
- 1 teaspoon dehydrated onions
- ½ teaspoon poppy seeds
- ½ teaspoon garlic powder
- ½ teaspoon sea salt flakes

Directions:

1. In a large bowl, mix together the flour, baking powder, and salt. Make a well in the dough and add in the Greek yogurt. Mix with a spoon until a dough forms.
2. Place the dough onto a heavily floured surface and knead for 3 minutes. You may use up to 1 cup of additional flour as you knead the dough, if necessary.
3. Cut the dough into 8 pieces and roll each piece into a 15-cm, snakelike piece. Touch the ends of each piece together so it closes the circle and forms a bagel shape. Brush the tops of the bagels with the whisked egg.
4. In a small bowl, combine the sesame seeds, dehydrated onions, poppy seeds, garlic powder, and sea salt flakes. Sprinkle the seasoning on top of the bagels.
5. Preheat the air fryer to 180°C/360°F. Using a bench scraper or flat-edged spatula, carefully place the bagels into the air fryer basket. Spray the bagel tops with cooking spray. Air-fry the bagels for 6 minutes or until golden brown. Allow the bread to cool at least 10 minutes before slicing for serving.

Variations & Ingredients Tips:

▶ Use whole wheat flour for a more nutritious bagel.
▶ Add dried herbs like rosemary or thyme to the seasoning mix.
▶ Top with cream cheese or your favorite bagel spread.

Per Serving: Calories: 264; Total Fat: 3.5g; Saturated Fat: 1.1g; Cholesterol: 51mg; Sodium: 609mg; Total Carbohydrates: 44.9g; Dietary Fiber: 1.6g; Total Sugars: 2.8g; Protein: 11.7g

Egg Muffins

Servings: 4 | Prep Time: 5 Minutes | Cooking Time: 11 Minutes

Ingredients:

- 4 eggs
- salt and pepper
- olive oil
- 4 English muffins, split
- 1 cup shredded Colby Jack cheese
- 4 slices ham or Canadian bacon

Directions:

1. Preheat air fryer to 200°C/390°F.
2. Beat together eggs and add salt and pepper to taste. Spray air fryer baking pan lightly with oil and add eggs. Cook for 2 minutes, stir, and continue cooking for 4 minutes, stirring every minute, until eggs are scrambled to your preference. Remove pan from air fryer.
3. Place bottom halves of English muffins in air fryer basket. Take half of the shredded cheese and divide it among the muffins. Top each with a slice of ham and one-quarter of the eggs. Sprinkle remaining cheese on top of the eggs. Use a fork to press the cheese into the egg a little so it doesn't slip off before it melts.
4. Cook at 180°C/360°F for 1 minute. Add English muffin tops and cook for 4 minutes to heat through and toast the muffins.

Variations & Ingredients Tips:

▶ Use bagels, croissants or biscuits instead of English muffins.
▶ Add some sliced avocado, tomato or baby spinach on top.
▶ Drizzle with hot sauce or salsa for a spicy kick.

Per Serving: Calories: 391; Total Fat: 21g; Saturated Fat: 10g; Cholesterol: 240mg; Sodium: 895mg; Total Carbs: 28g; Dietary Fiber: 2g; Total Sugars: 1g; Protein: 23g

Apple-cinnamon-walnut Muffins

Servings: 8 | Prep Time: 15 Minutes | Cooking Time: 11 Minutes

Ingredients:

- 1 cup flour
- ⅓ cup sugar
- 1 teaspoon baking powder
- ¼ teaspoon baking soda
- ¼ teaspoon salt
- 1 teaspoon cinnamon
- ¼ teaspoon ginger
- ¼ teaspoon nutmeg
- 1 egg
- 2 tablespoons pancake syrup, plus 2 teaspoons
- 2 tablespoons melted butter, plus 2 teaspoons
- ¾ cup unsweetened applesauce
- ½ teaspoon vanilla extract
- ¼ cup chopped walnuts
- ¼ cup diced apple
- 8 foil muffin cups, liners removed and sprayed with cooking spray

Directions:

1. Preheat air fryer to 165°C/330°F.
2. In a large bowl, stir together flour, sugar, baking powder, baking soda, salt, cinnamon, ginger, and nutmeg.
3. In a small bowl, beat egg until frothy. Add syrup, butter, applesauce, and vanilla and mix well.
4. Pour egg mixture into dry ingredients and stir just until moistened.
5. Gently stir in nuts and diced apple.
6. Divide batter among the 8 muffin cups.
7. Place 4 muffin cups in air fryer basket and cook at 165°C/330°F for 11 minutes.
8. Repeat with remaining 4 muffins or until toothpick inserted in center comes out clean.

Variations & Ingredients Tips:

▶ Substitute whole wheat flour for part of the all-purpose flour
▶ Add raisins or other dried fruit
▶ Use muffin liners instead of foil cups

Per Serving: Calories: 175; Total Fat: 7g; Saturated Fat: 2g; Cholesterol: 30mg; Sodium: 180mg; Total Carbs: 26g; Dietary Fiber: 2g; Total Sugars: 13g; Protein: 3g

Appetizers And Snacks

Cheesy Pigs In A Blanket

Servings: 4 | Prep Time: 15 Minutes | Cooking Time: 7 Minutes

Ingredients:

- 24 cocktail size smoked sausages
- 6 slices deli-sliced Cheddar cheese, each cut into 8 rectangular pieces
- 1 (225 g) tube refrigerated crescent roll dough
- ketchup or mustard for dipping

Directions:

1. Unroll the crescent roll dough into one large sheet. If your crescent roll dough has perforated seams, pinch or roll all the perforated seams together. Cut the large sheet of dough into 4 rectangles. Then cut each rectangle into 6 pieces by making one slice lengthwise in the middle and 2 slices horizontally. You should have 24 pieces of dough.
2. Make a deep slit lengthwise down the center of the cocktail sausage. Stuff two pieces of cheese into the slit in the sausage. Roll one piece of crescent dough around the stuffed cocktail sausage leaving the ends of the sausage exposed. Pinch the seam together. Repeat with the remaining sausages.
3. Preheat the air fryer to 175°C/350°F.
4. Air-fry in 2 batches, placing the sausages seam side down in the basket. Air-fry for 7 minutes. Serve hot with ketchup or your favorite mustard for dipping.

Variations & Ingredients Tips:

- Use bratwurst or Italian sausage instead of smoked sausage.
- Stuff with pepper jack or mozzarella cheese for different flavors.
- Brush with melted butter and sprinkle with everything bagel seasoning before cooking.

Per Serving: Calories: 469; Total Fat: 37g; Saturated Fat: 14g; Cholesterol: 55mg; Sodium: 1315mg; Total Carbs: 21g; Dietary Fiber: 0g; Total Sugars: 6g; Protein: 16g

Rich Clam Spread

Servings: 6 | Prep Time: 15 Minutes | Cooking Time: 40 Minutes

Ingredients:

- 2 cans chopped clams in clam juice
- ⅓ cup panko bread crumbs
- 1 garlic clove, minced
- 1 tbsp olive oil
- 1 tbsp lemon juice
- ¼ tsp hot sauce
- 1 tsp Worcestershire sauce
- ½ tsp shallot powder
- ¼ tsp dried dill
- Salt and pepper to taste
- ½ tsp sweet paprika
- 4 tsp grated Parmesan cheese
- 2 celery stalks, chopped

Directions:

1. Completely drain one can of clams. Add them to a bowl along with the entire can of clams, breadcrumbs, garlic, olive oil, lemon juice, Worcestershire sauce, hot sauce, shallot powder, dill, pepper, salt, paprika, and 2 tbsp Parmesan. Combine well and set aside for 10 minutes. After that time, put the mixture in a greased baking dish. Preheat air fryer to 165°C/325°F. Put the dish in the air fryer and bake for 10 minutes. Sprinkle the remaining paprika and Parmesan, and continue to cook until golden brown on top, 8-10 minutes. Serve hot along with celery sticks.

Variations & Ingredients Tips:

- Add chopped bacon, sun-dried tomatoes, or artichoke hearts for extra flavor and texture.
- Serve with crackers, baguette slices, or pita chips for dipping.
- For a spicier version, increase the amount of hot sauce or add a pinch of cayenne pepper.

Per Serving: Calories: 99; Total Fat: 4g; Saturated Fat: 1g; Cholesterol: 16mg; Sodium: 312mg; Total Carbs: 8g;

Dietary Fiber: 1g; Total Sugars: 1g; Protein: 7g

Spicy Sweet Potato Tater-tots

Servings: 6 | Prep Time: 10 Minutes | Cooking Time: 10 Minutes

Ingredients:

- 1.5 L filtered water
- 2 medium sweet potatoes, peeled and cut in half
- 1 tsp garlic powder
- ½ tsp black pepper, divided
- ½ tsp salt, divided
- 1 cup panko breadcrumbs
- 1 tsp blackened seasoning

Directions:

1. In a large stovetop pot, bring the water to a boil. Add the sweet potatoes and let boil about 10 minutes, until a metal fork prong can be inserted but the potatoes still have a slight give (not completely mashed). Carefully remove the potatoes from the pot and let cool. When you're able to touch them, grate the potatoes into a large bowl. Mix the garlic powder, ¼ teaspoon of the black pepper, and ¼ teaspoon of the salt into the potatoes. Place the mixture in the refrigerator and let set at least 45 minutes (if you're leaving them longer than 45 minutes, cover the bowl). Before assembling, mix the breadcrumbs and blackened seasoning in a small bowl. Remove the sweet potatoes from the refrigerator and preheat the air fryer to 200°C/400°F. Assemble the tater-tots by using a teaspoon to portion batter evenly and form into a tater-tot shape. Roll each tater-tot in the breadcrumb mixture. Then carefully place the tater-tots in the air fryer basket. Be sure that you've liberally sprayed the air fryer basket with an olive oil mist. Repeat until tater-tots fill the basket without touching one another. You'll need to do multiple batches, depending on the size of your air fryer. Cook the tater-tots for 3 to 6 minutes, flip, and cook another 3 to 6 minutes. Remove from the air fryer carefully and keep warm until ready to serve.

Variations & Ingredients Tips:

- Add grated Parmesan cheese, chopped herbs, or red pepper flakes to the breadcrumb mixture for extra flavor.
- Serve with chipotle mayo, sriracha ketchup, or garlic aioli for dipping.
- Make a large batch and freeze the uncooked tater-tots for a quick and easy snack or side dish later.

Per Serving: Calories: 152; Total Fat: 2g; Saturated Fat: 0g; Sodium: 331mg; Total Carbohydrates: 30g; Dietary Fiber: 3g; Total Sugars: 5g; Protein: 3g

Maple Loaded Sweet Potatoes

Servings: 4 | Prep Time: 5 Minutes | Cooking Time: 45 Minutes

Ingredients:

- 4 sweet potatoes
- 2 tbsp butter
- 2 tbsp maple syrup
- 1 tsp cinnamon
- 1 tsp lemon zest
- ½ tsp vanilla extract

Directions:

1. Preheat air fryer to 200°C/390°F. Poke three holes on the top of each sweet potato using a fork. Arrange sweet potatoes in the air fryer and bake for 40 minutes. Remove and let cool for 5 minutes. While the sweet potatoes cool, melt butter and maple syrup together in the microwave for 15-20 seconds. Remove from microwave and stir in cinnamon, lemon zest, and vanilla. When the sweet potatoes are cool enough to handle, cut them open and drizzle the cinnamon butter mixture over each. Serve immediately and enjoy your Maple Loaded Sweet Potatoes!

Variations & Ingredients Tips:

- For a nuttier flavor, add a handful of chopped pecans or walnuts to the butter mixture.
- Substitute honey for the maple syrup if desired.
- For a savory twist, add a pinch of cayenne pepper or smoked paprika to the butter.

Per Serving: Calories: 237; Total Fat: 6g; Saturated Fat: 4g; Cholesterol: 15mg; Sodium: 73mg; Total Carbs: 44g; Dietary Fiber: 5g; Total Sugars: 19g; Protein: 3g

Spiced Parsnip Chips

Servings: 2 | Prep Time: 10 Minutes | Cooking Time: 35 Minutes

Ingredients:

- ½ tsp smoked paprika
- ¼ tsp chili powder
- ¼ tsp garlic powder
- ⅛ tsp onion powder
- ⅛ tsp cayenne pepper
- ⅛ tsp granulated sugar
- 1 tsp salt
- 1 parsnip, cut into chips
- 2 tsp olive oil

Directions:

1. Preheat air fryer to 200°C/400°F. Mix all spices in a bowl and reserve. In another bowl, combine parsnip chips, olive oil, and salt. Place parsnip chips in the lightly greased frying basket and air fry for 12 minutes, shaking once. Transfer the chips to a bowl, toss in seasoning mix, and let sit for 15 minutes before serving.

Variations & Ingredients Tips:

- Try using different root vegetables like carrots, beets, or sweet potatoes for colorful chips.
- Add grated Parmesan cheese or nutritional yeast to the seasoning mix for a cheesy flavor.
- Serve with your favorite dip like ranch dressing, hummus, or guacamole.

Per Serving: Calories: 122; Total Fat: 7g; Saturated Fat: 1g; Sodium: 1192mg; Total Carbohydrates: 15g; Dietary Fiber: 4g; Total Sugars: 4g; Protein: 1g

Crab Toasts

Servings: 15 | Prep Time: 10 Minutes | Cooking Time: 5 Minutes

Ingredients:

- 1 170 g can flaked crabmeat, well drained
- 3 tablespoons light mayonnaise
- ½ teaspoon lemon juice
- 1 teaspoon Worcestershire sauce
- ¼ cup shredded sharp Cheddar cheese
- ¼ cup shredded Parmesan cheese
- 1 loaf artisan bread, French bread, or baguette, cut into slices 10 mm thick

Directions:

1. Mix together all ingredients except the bread slices.
2. Spread each slice of bread with a thin layer of crabmeat mixture. (For a bread slice measuring 5 x 4 cm you will need about ½ tablespoon of crab mixture.)
3. Place in air fryer basket in single layer and cook at 180°C/360°F for 5 minutes or until tops brown and toast is crispy.
4. Repeat step 3 to cook remaining crab toasts.

Variations & Ingredients Tips:

- Use smoked salmon, cooked shrimp or lobster instead of crab.
- Add some minced jalapeños or hot sauce to the mixture for a spicy kick.
- Sprinkle with Old Bay seasoning or smoked paprika before cooking.

Per Serving: Calories: 104; Total Fat: 4g; Saturated Fat: 1g; Cholesterol: 17mg; Sodium: 271mg; Total Carbs: 12g; Dietary Fiber: 1g; Total Sugars: 1g; Protein: 5g

Cinnamon Pita Chips

Servings: 4 | Prep Time: 5 Minutes | Cooking Time: 6 Minutes

Ingredients:

- 2 tablespoons sugar
- 2 teaspoons cinnamon
- 2 whole 15 cm pitas, whole grain or white
- oil for misting or cooking spray

Directions:

1. Mix sugar and cinnamon together.
2. Cut each pita in half and each half into 4 wedges. Break apart each wedge at the fold.
3. Mist one side of pita wedges with oil or cooking spray. Sprinkle them all with half of the cinnamon sugar.
4. Turn the wedges over, mist the other side with oil or cooking spray, and sprinkle with the remaining cinnamon sugar.
5. Place pita wedges in air fryer basket and cook at 165°C/330°F for 2 minutes.
6. Shake basket and cook 2 more minutes. Shake again, and if needed cook 2 more minutes, until crisp. Watch carefully because at this point they will cook very quickly.

Variations & Ingredients Tips:

- Use flavored pita bread like garlic or sun-dried tomato for extra flavor.
- Substitute pumpkin pie spice or apple pie spice for the cinnamon.
- Serve with fruit salsa or vanilla yogurt dip.

Per Serving: Calories: 134; Total Fat: 1g; Saturated Fat: 0g; Cholesterol: 0mg; Sodium: 217mg; Total Carbs: 29g; Dietary Fiber: 2g; Total Sugars: 7g; Protein: 4g

Cherry Chipotle Bbq Chicken Wings

Servings: 2 | Prep Time: 10 Minutes | Cooking Time: 12 Minutes

Ingredients:

- 1 teaspoon smoked paprika
- ½ teaspoon dry mustard powder
- 1 teaspoon dried oregano
- 1 teaspoon dried thyme
- ½ teaspoon chili powder
- 1 teaspoon salt
- 900 g chicken wings
- vegetable oil or spray
- salt and freshly ground black pepper
- 1 to 2 tablespoons chopped chipotle peppers in adobo sauce
- 80 ml cherry preserves ¼ cup tomato ketchup

Directions:

1. Combine the first six ingredients in a large bowl. Prepare the chicken wings by cutting off the wing tips and discarding (or freezing for chicken stock). Divide the drumettes from the win-gettes by cutting through the joint. Place the chicken wing pieces in the bowl with the spice mix. Toss or shake well to coat.
2. Preheat the air fryer to 200°C/400°F.
3. Spray the wings lightly with the vegetable oil and air-fry the wings in two batches for 10 minutes per batch, shaking the basket halfway through the cooking process. When both batches are done, toss all the wings back into the basket for another 2 minutes to heat through and finish cooking.
4. While the wings are air-frying, combine the chopped chipotle peppers, cherry preserves and ketchup in a bowl.
5. Remove the wings from the air fryer, toss them in the cherry chipotle BBQ sauce and serve with napkins!

Variations & Ingredients Tips:

- Use peach or apricot preserves instead of cherry for a different flavor.
- Add some honey or brown sugar to the sauce for extra sweetness.

- Serve with blue cheese or ranch dressing on the side for dipping.

Per Serving: Calories: 731; Total Fat: 45g; Saturated Fat: 13g; Cholesterol: 194mg; Sodium: 2424mg; Total Carbs: 36g; Dietary Fiber: 1g; Total Sugars: 28g; Protein: 45g

Shrimp Toasts

Servings: 4 | Prep Time: 15 Minutes | Cooking Time: 8 Minutes

Ingredients:

- 225 g raw shrimp, peeled and de-veined
- 1 egg (or 2 egg whites)
- 2 scallions, plus more for garnish
- 2 teaspoons grated fresh ginger
- 1 teaspoon soy sauce
- ½ teaspoon toasted sesame oil
- 2 tablespoons chopped fresh cilantro or parsley
- 1 to 2 teaspoons sriracha sauce
- 6 slices thinly-sliced white sandwich bread (Pepperidge Farm®)
- ½ cup sesame seeds
- Thai chili sauce

Directions:

1. Combine the shrimp, egg, scallions, fresh ginger, soy sauce, sesame oil, cilantro (or parsley) and sriracha sauce in a food processor and process into a chunky paste, scraping down the sides of the food processor bowl as necessary.
2. Cut the crusts off the sandwich bread and generously spread the shrimp paste onto each slice of bread. Place the sesame seeds on a plate and invert each shrimp toast into the sesame seeds to coat, pressing down gently. Cut each slice of bread into 4 triangles.
3. Preheat the air fryer to 200°C/400°F.
4. Transfer one layer of shrimp toast triangles to the air fryer and air-fry at 200°C/400°F for 8 minutes, or until the sesame seeds are toasted on top.
5. Serve warm with a little Thai chili sauce and some sliced scallions as garnish.

Variations & Ingredients Tips:

- Use whole wheat or multigrain bread for a healthier version.
- Replace the sesame seeds with black sesame seeds, poppy seeds, or everything bagel seasoning for a dif-

ferent flavor and appearance.
- Make a vegetarian version by replacing the shrimp with finely chopped mushrooms or water chestnuts.

Per Serving: Calories: 235; Total Fat: 9g; Saturated Fat: 2g; Cholesterol: 145mg; Sodium: 510mg; Total Carbs: 20g; Fiber: 2g; Sugars: 2g; Protein: 17g

Basil Feta Crostini

Servings: 4 | Prep Time: 5 Minutes | Cooking Time: 10 Minutes

Ingredients:

- 1 baguette, sliced
- ¼ cup olive oil
- 2 garlic cloves, minced
- 113 g feta cheese
- 2 tbsp basil, minced

Directions:

1. Preheat air fryer to 190°C/380°F. Combine together the olive oil and garlic in a bowl. Brush it over one side of each slice of bread. Put the bread in a single layer in the frying basket and Bake for 5 minutes. In a small bowl, mix together the feta cheese and basil. Remove the toast from the air fryer, then spread a thin layer of the feta cheese mixture over the top of each piece. Serve.

Variations & Ingredients Tips:

- Use goat cheese or ricotta instead of feta for a milder flavor.
- Top with diced tomatoes or roasted red peppers for added color and taste.
- Drizzle with balsamic glaze or honey before serving.

Per Serving: Calories: 364; Total Fat: 19g; Saturated Fat: 7g; Cholesterol: 33mg; Sodium: 674mg; Total Carbs: 38g; Dietary Fiber: 1g; Total Sugars: 1g; Protein: 11g

Beer-battered Onion Rings

Servings: 4 | Prep Time: 10 Minutes | Cooking Time: 25 Minutes

Ingredients:

- 2 sliced onions, rings separated
- 1 cup flour
- Salt and pepper to taste
- 1 tsp garlic powder
- 1 cup beer

Directions:

1. Preheat air fryer to 175°C/350°F. In a mixing bowl, combine the flour, garlic powder, beer, salt, and black pepper. Dip the onion rings into the bowl and lay the coated rings in the frying basket. Air Fry for 15 minutes, shaking the basket several times during cooking to jostle the onion rings and ensure a good even fry. Once ready, the onions should be crispy and golden brown. Serve hot.

Variations & Ingredients Tips:

- Use panko breadcrumbs for an extra crispy coating.
- Substitute buttermilk or seltzer water for the beer.
- Sprinkle with Parmesan cheese or everything bagel seasoning after cooking.

Per Serving: Calories: 190; Total Fat: 1g; Saturated Fat: 0g; Cholesterol: 0mg; Sodium: 10mg; Total Carbs: 38g; Dietary Fiber: 2g; Total Sugars: 4g; Protein: 5g

Roasted Tomatillo Salsa

Servings: 4 | Prep Time: 10 Minutes | Cooking Time: 35 Minutes + Cooling Time

Ingredients:

- 2 tbsp olive oil
- 1 serrano pepper
- 1 jalapeño pepper
- ¼ white onion
- 2 garlic cloves
- 340 g tomatillos
- 3 tbsp chopped cilantro
- ¼ tsp sugar
- Salt to taste

Directions:

1. Preheat air fryer to 200°C/400°F. Lightly drizzle the serrano, jalapeño, onion and garlic with some olive oil. Bake in the air fryer for 14 minutes, flipping them once until charred. Remove the peppers to a foil, wrap and let cool for 10 minutes. Put the rest of the veggies into a food processor. Lightly brush the tomatillos with the remaining olive oil. Cook in the air fryer for 10 minutes, flipping the tomatillos once until charred. Transfer the tomatillos to your food processor. Unwrap the peppers. Peel off the skin and remove all of the seeds. Transfer

to the food processor. Also, add cilantro, sugar, and salt. Pulse until coarsely chopped. Slowly add 5-6 tbsp of water until smooth and pureed. Serve.

Variations & Ingredients Tips:

- Add lime juice, cumin, or oregano for extra flavor.
- Roast a few cloves of garlic along with the vegetables for a deeper, richer taste.
- Adjust the amount of serrano and jalapeño peppers to make the salsa milder or spicier.

Per Serving: Calories: 101; Total Fat: 7g; Saturated Fat: 1g; Cholesterol: 0mg; Sodium: 9mg; Total Carbs: 9g; Dietary Fiber: 2g; Total Sugars: 5g; Protein: 1g

Thai-style Crab Wontons

Servings: 4 | Prep Time: 20 Minutes | Cooking Time: 20 Minutes

Ingredients:

- 115 g cottage cheese, softened
- 70 g lump crabmeat
- 2 scallions, chopped
- 2 garlic cloves, minced
- 2 tsp tamari sauce
- 12 wonton wrappers
- 1 egg white, beaten
- 5 tbsp Thai sweet chili sauce

Directions:

1. Using a fork, mix together cottage cheese, crabmeat, scallions, garlic, and tamari sauce in a bowl. Set it near your workspace along with a small bowl of water. Place one wonton wrapper on a clean surface. The points should be facing so that it looks like a diamond. Put 1 level tbsp of the crab and cheese mix onto the center of the wonton wrapper. Dip your finger into the water and run the moist finger along the edges of the wrapper. Fold one corner of the wrapper to the opposite side and make a triangle. From the center out, press out any air and seal the edges. Continue this process until all of the wontons have been filled and sealed. Brush both sides of the wontons with beaten egg white. Preheat air fryer to 170°C/340°F. Place the wontons on the bottom of the greased frying basket in a single layer. Bake for 8 minutes, flipping the wontons once until golden brown and crispy. Serve hot and enjoy!

Variations & Ingredients Tips:

- Substitute crab with cooked, shredded chicken, pork, or shrimp for a different filling.
- Add finely chopped water chestnuts, bamboo shoots, or mushrooms for extra crunch and flavor.
- Serve with hoisin sauce, soy sauce, or plum sauce for dipping.

Per Serving: Calories: 204; Total Fat: 4g; Saturated Fat: 1g; Cholesterol: 37mg; Sodium: 648mg; Total Carbohydrates: 29g; Dietary Fiber: 1g; Total Sugars: 10g; Protein: 12g

Fried Goat Cheese

Servings: 3 | Prep Time: 40 Minutes | Cooking Time: 4 Minutes

Ingredients:

- 200 g 2.5 to 4 cm diameter goat cheese log
- 2 Large egg(s)
- 1¾ cups Plain dried bread crumbs (gluten-free, if a concern)
- Vegetable oil spray

Directions:

1. Slice the goat cheese log into 13 mm thick rounds. Set these flat on a small cutting board, a small baking sheet, or a large plate. Freeze uncovered for 30 minutes.
2. Preheat the air fryer to 200°C/400°F.
3. Set up and fill two shallow soup plates or small pie plates on your counter: one in which you whisk the egg(s) until uniform and the other for the bread crumbs.
4. Take the goat cheese rounds out of the freezer. With clean, dry hands, dip one round in the egg(s) to coat it on all sides. Let the excess egg slip back into the rest, then dredge the round in the bread crumbs, turning it to coat all sides, even the edges. Repeat this process—egg, then bread crumbs—for a second coating. Coat both sides of the round and its edges with vegetable oil spray, then set it aside. Continue double-dipping, double-dredging, and spraying the remaining rounds.
5. Place the rounds in one layer in the basket. Air-fry undisturbed for 4 minutes, or until lightly browned and crunchy. Do not overcook. Some of the goat cheese may break through the crust. A few little breaks are fine but stop the cooking before the coating reaches structural failure.
6. Remove the basket from the machine and set aside for 3 minutes. Use a nonstick-safe spatula, and maybe a

flatware fork for balance, to transfer the rounds to a wire rack. Cool for 5 minutes more before serving.

Variations & Ingredients Tips:

- Use brie, camembert or feta instead of goat cheese.
- Roll the breaded rounds in chopped nuts, herbs or seeds before air frying.
- Serve with honey, fig jam or cranberry sauce for dipping.

Per Serving: Calories: 490; Total Fat: 24g; Saturated Fat: 12g; Cholesterol: 174mg; Sodium: 935mg; Total Carbs: 44g; Dietary Fiber: 3g; Total Sugars: 5g; Protein: 26g

Mouth-watering Vegetable Casserole

Servings: 3 | Prep Time: 10 Minutes | Cooking Time: 45 Minutes

Ingredients:

- 1 red bell pepper, chopped
- 225-g okra, trimmed
- 1 red onion, chopped
- 400 g can diced tomatoes
- 2 tbsp balsamic vinegar
- 1 tbsp allspice
- 1 tsp ground cumin
- 1 cup baby spinach

Directions:

1. Preheat air fryer to 200°C/400°F. Combine the bell pepper, red onion, okra, tomatoes and juices, balsamic vinegar, allspice, and cumin in a baking pan and roast for 25 minutes, stirring every 10 minutes. Stir in spinach and roast for another 5 minutes. Serve warm.

Variations & Ingredients Tips:

- Add other vegetables like zucchini, eggplant, or mushrooms for variety.
- Use fresh tomatoes instead of canned when they're in season.
- Top with crumbled feta cheese or toasted pine nuts before serving.

Per Serving: Calories: 122; Total Fat: 2g; Saturated Fat: 0g; Cholesterol: no data; Sodium: 421mg; Total Carbs: 24g; Dietary Fiber: 7g; Total Sugars: 12g; Protein: 5g

Sausage & Cauliflower Balls

Servings: 4 | Prep Time: 20 Minutes | Cooking Time: 30 Minutes

Ingredients:

- 2 chicken sausage links, casings removed
- 1 cup shredded Monterey jack cheese
- 4 1/2 cups (680g) riced cauliflower
- 1/2 tsp salt
- 1 1/4 cups pizza sauce, divided
- 2 eggs
- 1/2 cup breadcrumbs
- 3 tsp grated Parmesan cheese

Directions:

1. In a large skillet over high heat, cook the sausages while breaking them up into smaller pieces with a spoon. Cook through completely for 4 minutes. Add cauliflower, salt, and 1/4 cup of pizza sauce. Lower heat to medium and stir-fry for 7 minutes or until the cauliflower is tender. Remove from heat and stir in Monterey cheese. Allow to cool slightly, 4 minutes or until it is easy to handle. Lightly coat a 1/4-cup measuring cup with cooking spray. Pack and level the cup with the cauliflower mixture. Remove from the cup and roll it into a ball in your palm. Set aside and repeat until you have 12 balls. In a bowl, beat eggs and 1 tbsp of water until combined. In another bowl, combine breadcrumbs and Parmesan. Dip one cauliflower ball into the egg mixture, then in the crumbs. Press the crumbs so that they stick to the ball. Put onto a workspace and spray with cooking oil. Repeat for all balls. Preheat air fryer to 400°F/200°C. Place the balls on the bottom of the frying basket in a single layer. Air Fry for about 8-10 minutes, flipping once until the crumbs are golden and the balls are hot throughout. Warm up the remaining 1 cup pizza sauce as a dip.

Variations & Ingredients Tips:

- Substitute Italian sausage for a spicier version.
- Use panko breadcrumbs for an extra crispy exterior.
- Bake in the oven at 400°F/200°C for 15-18 minutes if no air fryer.

Per Serving (3 balls): Calories: 305; Total Fat: 15g; Saturated Fat: 6g; Cholesterol: 111mg; Sodium: 1089mg; Total Carbs: 26g; Dietary Fiber: 4g; Total Sugars: 5g; Protein: 18g

Sweet Potato Chips

Servings: 4 | Prep Time: 40 Minutes | Cooking Time: 10 Minutes

Ingredients:

- 2 medium sweet potatoes, washed
- 2 cups filtered water
- 1 tbsp avocado oil
- 2 tsp brown sugar
- ½ tsp salt

Directions:

1. Using a mandolin, slice the potatoes into 3-mm pieces. Add the water to a large bowl. Place the potatoes in the bowl, and soak for at least 30 minutes. Preheat the air fryer to 175°C/350°F. Drain the water and pat the chips dry with a paper towel or kitchen cloth. Toss the chips with the avocado oil, brown sugar, and salt. Liberally spray the air fryer basket with olive oil mist. Set the chips inside the air fryer, separating them so they're not on top of each other. Cook for 5 minutes, shake the basket, and cook another 5 minutes, or until browned. Remove and let cool a few minutes prior to serving. Repeat until all the chips are cooked.

Variations & Ingredients Tips:

- Use different types of potatoes like russet, Yukon Gold, or purple potatoes for varied flavors and colors.
- Season the chips with different spices like cinnamon, nutmeg, or pumpkin pie spice for a sweet twist.
- Serve with a dipping sauce like honey mustard, ranch, or garlic aioli.

Per Serving: Calories: 118; Total Fat: 4g; Saturated Fat: 1g; Sodium: 296mg; Total Carbohydrates: 20g; Dietary Fiber: 3g; Total Sugars: 6g; Protein: 1g

Jalapeño & Mozzarella Stuffed Mushrooms

Servings: 4 | Prep Time: 15 Minutes | Cooking Time: 30 Minutes

Ingredients:

- 16 button mushrooms
- 1/3 cup salsa
- 3 garlic cloves, minced
- 1 onion, finely chopped
- 1 jalapeño pepper, minced
- ⅛ tsp cayenne pepper
- 3 tbsp shredded mozzarella
- 2 tsp olive oil

Directions:

1. Preheat air fryer to 177°C/350°F. Remove the stem from the mushrooms, then finely slice them. Set the caps aside. Combine the salsa, garlic, onion, jalapeño, cayenne, and mozzarella cheese in a bowl, then add the stems. Fill the mushroom caps with the mixture, making sure to overfill so the mix is coming out of the top. Drizzle with olive oil. Place the caps in the air fryer and bake for 8-12 minutes. The filling should be hot and the mushrooms soft. Serve warm.

Variations & Ingredients Tips:

- Use kalamata olives, black olives or a mix of different varieties.
- Add some grated Parmesan cheese or lemon zest to the breading.
- Serve as a garnish for martinis or Bloody Marys.

Per Serving: Calories: 193; Total Fat: 11g; Saturated Fat: 2g; Cholesterol: 12mg; Sodium: 525mg; Total Carbs: 19g; Dietary Fiber: 2g; Total Sugars: 1g; Protein: 4g

Thyme Sweet Potato Chips

Servings: 2 | Prep Time: 10 Minutes | Cooking Time: 20 Minutes

Ingredients:

- 1 tbsp olive oil
- 1 sweet potato, sliced
- ¼ tsp dried thyme
- Salt to taste

Directions:

1. Preheat air fryer to 200°C/390°F. Spread the sweet potato slices in the greased basket and brush with olive oil. Air fry for 6 minutes. Remove the basket, shake, and sprinkle with thyme and salt. Cook for 6 more minutes or until lightly browned. Serve warm and enjoy!

Variations & Ingredients Tips:

- Experiment with different herbs and spices like rosemary, paprika, or garlic powder.
- Use russet potatoes, parsnips, or beets for a variety of homemade chips.

- Serve with your favorite dip like ranch dressing, hummus, or French onion dip.

Per Serving: Calories: 142; Total Fat: 7g; Saturated Fat: 1g; Sodium: 201mg; Total Carbohydrates: 19g; Dietary Fiber: 3g; Total Sugars: 5g; Protein: 2g

Potato Samosas

Servings: 12 | Prep Time: 30 Minutes | Cooking Time: 10 Minutes

Ingredients:

- ¾ cup instant mashed potato flakes
- ¾ cup boiling water
- ⅓ cup plain full-fat or low-fat yogurt (not Greek yogurt or fat-free yogurt)
- 1 tsp yellow curry powder, purchased or homemade (see here)
- ½ tsp table salt
- 1½ purchased refrigerated pie crusts, from a minimum 400-g box
- All-purpose flour
- Vegetable oil spray

Directions:

1. Put the potato flakes in a medium bowl and pour the boiling water over them. Stir well to form a mixture like thick mashed potatoes. Cool for 15 minutes. Preheat the air fryer to 200°C/400°F. Stir the yogurt, curry powder, and salt into the potato mixture until smooth and uniform. Unwrap and unroll the sheet(s) of pie crust dough onto a clean, dry work surface. Cut out as many 10-cm circles as you can with a big cookie cutter or a giant sturdy water glass, or even by tracing the circle with the rim of a 10-cm plate. Gather up the scraps of dough. Lightly flour your work surface and set the scraps on top. Roll them together into a sheet that matches the thickness of the original crusts and cut more circles until you have the number you need—8 circles for the small batch, 12 for the medium batch, or 16 for the large. Pick up one of the circles and create something like an ice cream cone by folding and sealing the circle together so that it is closed at the bottom and flared open at the top, in a conical shape. Put 1 tablespoon of the potato filling into the open cone, then push the filling into the cone toward the point. Fold the top over the filling and press to seal the dough into a triangular shape with corners, taking care to seal those corners all around. Set aside and continue forming and filling the remainder of the dough circles as directed. Lightly coat the filled dough pockets with vegetable oil spray on all sides. Set them in the basket in one layer and air-fry undisturbed for 10 minutes, or until lightly browned and crisp. Gently turn the contents of the basket out onto a wire rack. Use kitchen tongs to gently set all the samosas seam side up. Cool for 10 minutes before serving.

Variations & Ingredients Tips:

- Add finely chopped onions, peas, or carrots to the potato mixture for extra flavor and texture.
- Serve with tamarind chutney or mint-cilantro chutney for dipping.
- Make a sweet version by filling the samosas with sweetened ricotta cheese and raisins or chocolate chips.

Per Serving: Calories: 133; Total Fat: 7g; Saturated Fat: 2g; Cholesterol: 4mg; Sodium: 214mg; Total Carbs: 15g; Dietary Fiber: 1g; Total Sugars: 1g; Protein: 2g

Poultry Recipes

Philly Chicken Cheesesteak Stromboli

Servings: 2 | Prep Time: 30 Minutes | Cooking Time: 28 Minutes

Ingredients:

- ½ onion, sliced
- 1 teaspoon vegetable oil
- 2 boneless, skinless chicken breasts, partially frozen and sliced very thin on the bias (about 450g)
- 1 tablespoon Worcestershire sauce
- Salt and freshly ground black pepper
- ½ recipe of Blue Jean Chef pizza dough, or 400g of store-bought pizza dough
- 1½ cups grated Cheddar cheese
- ½ cup Cheese Whiz® (or other jarred cheese sauce), warmed gently in the microwave
- Tomato ketchup for serving

Directions:

1. Preheat the air fryer to 200°C/400°F.
2. Toss the sliced onion with oil and air-fry for 8 minutes, stirring halfway through the cooking time. Add the sliced chicken and Worcestershire sauce to the air fryer basket, and toss to evenly distribute the ingredients. Season the mixture with salt and freshly ground black pepper and air-fry for 8 minutes, stirring a couple of times during the cooking process. Remove the chicken and onion from the air fryer and let the mixture cool a little.
3. On a lightly floured surface, roll or press the pizza dough out into a 33-cm by 28-cm rectangle, with the long side closest to you. Sprinkle half of the Cheddar cheese over the dough leaving an empty 2.5-cm border from the edge farthest away from you. Top the cheese with the chicken and onion mixture, spreading it out evenly. Drizzle the cheese sauce over the meat and sprinkle the remaining Cheddar cheese on top.
4. Start rolling the stromboli away from you and toward the empty border. Make sure the filling stays tightly tucked inside the roll. Finally, tuck the ends of the dough in and pinch the seam shut. Place the seam side down and shape the Stromboli into a U-shape to fit in the air-fry basket. Cut 4 small slits with the tip of a sharp knife evenly in the top of the dough and lightly brush the stromboli with a little oil.
5. Preheat the air fryer to 190°C/370°F.
6. Spray or brush the air fryer basket with oil and transfer the U-shaped stromboli to the air fryer basket. Air-fry for 12 minutes, turning the stromboli over halfway through the cooking time. (Use a plate to invert the stromboli out of the air fryer basket and then slide it back into the basket off the plate.)
7. To remove, carefully flip stromboli over onto a cutting board. Let it rest for a couple of minutes before serving. Slice the stromboli into 5-cm pieces and serve with ketchup for dipping, if desired.

Variations & Ingredients Tips:

▶ Use thinly sliced roast beef instead of chicken for a classic Philly cheesesteak.
▶ Add sautéed bell peppers and mushrooms to the filling.
▶ Brush the stromboli with garlic butter before air frying for extra flavor.

Per Serving: Calories: 970; Total Fat: 51g; Saturated Fat: 24g; Cholesterol: 210mg; Sodium: 1740mg; Total Carbs: 61g; Dietary Fiber: 3g; Total Sugars: 6g; Protein: 72g

Lemon Sage Roast Chicken

Servings: 4 | Prep Time: 15 Minutes | Cooking Time: 60 Minutes

Ingredients:

- 1 (1.8kg) chicken
- 1 bunch sage, divided
- 1 lemon, zest and juice
- Salt and freshly ground black pepper

Directions:

1. Preheat the air fryer to 175°C/350°F and pour a little water into the bottom of the air fryer drawer. (This will help prevent the grease that drips into the bottom drawer from burning and smoking.)
2. Run your fingers between the skin and flesh of the chicken breasts and thighs. Push a couple of sage leaves up underneath the skin of the chicken on each breast and each thigh.
3. Push some of the lemon zest up under the skin of the chicken next to the sage. Sprinkle some of the zest inside the chicken cavity, and reserve any leftover zest. Squeeze the lemon juice all over the chicken and in the cavity as well.
4. Season the chicken, inside and out, with the salt and freshly ground black pepper. Set a few sage leaves aside for the final garnish. Crumple up the remaining sage leaves and push them into the cavity of the chicken, along with one of the squeezed lemon halves.
5. Place the chicken breast side up into the air fryer basket and air-fry for 20 minutes at 175°C/350°F. Flip the chicken over so that it is breast side down and continue to air-fry for another 20 minutes. Return the chicken to breast side up and finish air-frying for 20 more minutes. The internal temperature of the chicken should register 74°C/165°F in the thickest part of the thigh when fully cooked.
6. Remove the chicken from the air fryer and let it rest on a cutting board for at least 5 minutes.
7. Cut the rested chicken into pieces, sprinkle with the reserved lemon zest and garnish with the reserved sage leaves.

Variations & Ingredients Tips:

- Add garlic cloves, thyme sprigs or rosemary to the cavity.
- Rub softened butter under the skin before cooking.
- Serve with a lemon-garlic pan sauce made from the drippings.

Per Serving: Calories: 540; Total Fat: 32g; Saturated Fat: 9g; Cholesterol: 185mg; Sodium: 330mg; Total Carbs: 2g; Dietary Fiber: 0g; Total Sugars: 0g; Protein: 60g

Crispy Duck With Cherry Sauce

Servings: 2 | Prep Time: 20 Minutes | Cooking Time: 33 Minutes

Ingredients:

- 1 whole duck (up to 2.3 kg), split in half, back and rib bones removed
- 1 teaspoon olive oil
- salt and freshly ground black pepper
- Cherry Sauce:
- 1 tablespoon butter
- 1 shallot, minced
- ½ cup sherry
- ¾ cup cherry preserves
- 1 cup chicken stock
- 1 teaspoon white wine vinegar
- 1 teaspoon fresh thyme leaves
- salt and freshly ground black pepper

Directions:

1. Preheat the air fryer to 200°C/400°F.
2. Trim some of the fat from the duck. Rub olive oil on the duck and season with salt and pepper. Place the duck halves in the air fryer basket, breast side up and facing the center of the basket.
3. Air-fry the duck for 20 minutes. Turn the duck over and air-fry for another 6 minutes.
4. While duck is air-frying, make the cherry sauce. Melt the butter in a large sauté pan. Add the shallot and sauté until it is just starting to brown – about 2 to 3 minutes. Add the sherry and deglaze the pan by scraping up any brown bits from the bottom of the pan. Simmer the liquid for a few minutes, until it has reduced by half. Add the cherry preserves, chicken stock and white wine vinegar. Whisk well to combine all the ingredients. Simmer the sauce until it thickens and coats the back of a spoon – about 5 to 7 minutes. Season with salt and pepper and stir in the fresh thyme leaves.
5. When the air fryer timer goes off, spoon some cherry sauce over the duck and continue to air-fry at 200°C/400°F for 4 more minutes. Then, turn the duck halves back over so that the breast side is facing up. Spoon more cherry sauce over the top of the duck, covering the skin completely. Air-fry for 3 more minutes and then remove the duck to a plate to rest for a few minutes.
6. Serve the duck in halves, or cut each piece in half again for a smaller serving. Spoon any additional sauce over the duck or serve it on the side.

Variations & Ingredients Tips:

- Use duck breasts or legs instead of a whole duck for quicker cooking time.
- Substitute cherry preserves with blackberry, raspberry, or apricot jam.
- Garnish with fresh herbs like rosemary, sage, or parsley before serving.

Per Serving: Calories: 610; Total Fat: 36g; Saturated Fat: 12g; Sodium: 430mg; Total Carbohydrates: 41g; Dietary Fiber: 1g; Total Sugars: 34g; Protein: 34g

Hawaiian Chicken

Servings: 4 | Prep Time: 10 Minutes | Cooking Time: 25 Minutes

Ingredients:

- 1 can (400g) diced pineapple
- 1 kiwi, sliced
- 2 tbsp coconut aminos
- 1 tbsp honey
- 3 garlic cloves, minced
- Salt and pepper to taste
- 1/2 tsp paprika
- 450g chicken breasts

Directions:

1. Preheat air fryer to 180°C/360°F.
2. Stir together pineapple, kiwi, coconut aminos, honey, garlic, salt, paprika, and pepper in a small bowl.
3. Arrange the chicken in a single layer in a baking dish. Spread half of the pineapple mixture over the top of the chicken. Transfer the dish into the frying basket.
4. Roast for 8 minutes, then flip the chicken. Spread the rest of the pineapple mixture over the top of the chicken and Roast for another 8-10 until the chicken is done.
5. Allow sitting for 5 minutes. Serve and enjoy!

Variations & Ingredients Tips:

- Use boneless, skinless chicken thighs for juicier meat.
- Add some red pepper flakes for a spicy kick.
- Garnish with chopped macadamia nuts and green onions.

Per Serving: Calories: 270; Total Fat: 4g; Saturated Fat: 1g; Cholesterol: 85mg; Sodium: 310mg; Total Carbs: 25g; Dietary Fiber: 2g; Total Sugars: 20g; Protein: 32g

Sweet Nutty Chicken Breasts

Servings: 4 | Prep Time: 10 Minutes | Cooking Time: 30 Minutes

Ingredients:

- 2 chicken breasts, halved lengthwise
- 1/4 cup honey mustard
- 1/4 cup chopped pecans
- 1 tbsp olive oil
- 1 tbsp parsley, chopped

Directions:

1. Preheat air fryer to 175°C/350°F.
2. Brush chicken breasts with honey mustard and olive oil on all sides.
3. Place the pecans in a bowl. Add and coat the chicken breasts.
4. Place the breasts in the greased frying basket and Air Fry for 25 minutes, turning once.
5. Let chill onto a serving plate for 5 minutes. Sprinkle with parsley and serve.

Variations & Ingredients Tips:

- Use other nuts like almonds or walnuts instead of pecans.
- Add dried herbs like thyme or rosemary to the nut coating.
- Serve with a honey mustard dipping sauce on the side.

Per Serving: Calories: 307; Total Fat: 14g; Saturated Fat: 2g; Cholesterol: 88mg; Sodium: 237mg; Total Carbs: 14g; Dietary Fiber: 1g; Total Sugars: 10g; Protein: 31g

Coconut Curry Chicken With Coconut Rice

Servings: 4 | Prep Time: 20 Minutes (plus Marinating Time) | Cooking Time: 56 Minutes

Ingredients:

- 1 (400-ml) can coconut milk
- 2 tablespoons green or red curry paste
- Zest and juice of one lime
- 1 clove garlic, minced
- 1 tablespoon grated fresh ginger
- 1 teaspoon ground cumin
- 1 (1.4 to 1.8-kg) chicken, cut into 8 pieces
- Vegetable or olive oil
- Salt and freshly ground black pepper
- Fresh cilantro leaves
- For the rice:
- 1 cup basmati or jasmine rice
- 1 cup water
- 1 cup coconut milk
- 1/2 teaspoon salt

- Freshly ground black pepper

Directions:

1. Make the marinade by combining the coconut milk, curry paste, lime zest and juice, garlic, ginger and cumin. Coat the chicken on all sides with the marinade and marinate the chicken for 1 hour to overnight in the refrigerator.
2. Preheat the air fryer to 190°C/380°F.
3. Brush the bottom of the air fryer basket with oil. Transfer the chicken thighs and drumsticks from the marinade to the air fryer basket, letting most of the marinade drip off. Season to taste with salt and freshly ground black pepper.
4. Air-fry the chicken drumsticks and thighs at 190°C/380°F for 12 minutes. Flip the chicken over and continue to air-fry for another 12 minutes. Set aside and air-fry the chicken breast pieces at 190°C/380°F for 15 minutes. Turn the chicken breast pieces over and air-fry for another 12 minutes. Return the chicken thighs and drumsticks to the air fryer and air-fry for an additional 5 minutes.
5. While the chicken is cooking, make the coconut rice. Rinse the rice kernels with water and drain well. Place the rice in a medium saucepan with a tight fitting lid, along with the water, coconut milk, salt and freshly ground black pepper. Bring the mixture to a boil and then cover, reduce the heat and let it cook gently for 20 minutes without lifting the lid. When the time is up, lift the lid, fluff with a fork and set aside.
6. Remove the chicken from the air fryer and serve warm with the coconut rice and fresh cilantro scattered around.

Variations & Ingredients Tips:

- Adjust the amount of curry paste to your spice preference.
- Use boneless, skinless chicken thighs for a quicker cooking time.
- Garnish with chopped peanuts or cashews for extra crunch.

Per Serving: Calories: 670; Total Fat: 42g; Saturated Fat: 29g; Cholesterol: 150mg; Sodium: 580mg; Total Carbs: 34g; Dietary Fiber: 1g; Total Sugars: 1g; Protein: 40g

Chicken Hand Pies

Servings: 8 | Prep Time: 20 Minutes | Cooking Time: 10 Minutes Per Batch

Ingredients:

- 3/4 cup chicken broth
- 3/4 cup frozen mixed peas and carrots
- 1 cup cooked chicken, chopped
- 1 tablespoon cornstarch
- 1 tablespoon milk
- Salt and pepper
- 1 8-count can organic flaky biscuits
- Oil for misting or cooking spray

Directions:

1. In a saucepan, bring broth to a boil. Add peas, carrots and chicken.
2. Mix cornstarch and milk, then stir into broth mixture until thickened.
3. Remove from heat, season with salt and pepper, and let cool slightly.
4. Separate biscuits into 16 rounds, flattening each slightly.
5. Place filling on 8 biscuit rounds. Top with remaining rounds and crimp edges sealed.
6. Mist both sides with oil or cooking spray.
7. Air fry in batches at 165°C/330°F for 10 minutes until golden brown.

Variations & Ingredients Tips:

- Use rotisserie or leftover chicken.
- Add diced potatoes, celery or onions to the filling.
- Brush with egg wash before cooking for a shiny finish.

Per Serving (2 hand pies): Calories: 312; Total Fat: 11g; Saturated Fat: 3g; Cholesterol: 38mg; Sodium: 779mg; Total Carbs: 41g; Dietary Fiber: 3g; Total Sugars: 4g; Protein: 13g

Nacho Chicken Fries

Servings: 4 | Prep Time: 15 Minutes | Cooking Time: 7 Minutes

Ingredients:

- 450g chicken tenders
- Salt
- 1/4 cup flour
- 2 eggs
- 3/4 cup panko breadcrumbs
- 3/4 cup crushed organic nacho cheese tortilla chips
- Oil for misting or cooking spray

- Seasoning Mix:
- 1 tablespoon chili powder
- 1 teaspoon ground cumin
- 1/2 teaspoon garlic powder
- 1/2 teaspoon onion powder

Directions:

1. Stir together all seasonings in a small cup and set aside.
2. Cut chicken tenders in half crosswise, then cut into strips no wider than about 1.25 cm.
3. Preheat air fryer to 200°C/390°F.
4. Salt chicken to taste. Place strips in large bowl and sprinkle with 1 tablespoon of the seasoning mix. Stir well to distribute seasonings.
5. Add flour to chicken and stir well to coat all sides.
6. Beat eggs together in a shallow dish.
7. In a second shallow dish, combine the panko, crushed chips, and the remaining 2 teaspoons of seasoning mix.
8. Dip chicken strips in eggs, then roll in crumbs. Mist with oil or cooking spray.
9. Chicken strips will cook best if done in two batches. They can be crowded and overlapping a little but not stacked in double or triple layers.
10. Cook for 4 minutes. Shake basket, mist with oil, and cook 3 more minutes, until chicken juices run clear and outside is crispy.
11. Repeat step 10 to cook remaining chicken fries.

Variations & Ingredients Tips:

- Use Cool Ranch Doritos or spicy nacho chips for different flavors.
- Dip chicken fries in queso, guacamole or salsa.
- Serve in tortillas with shredded lettuce, cheese and pico de gallo.

Per Serving: Calories: 360; Total Fat: 14g; Saturated Fat: 3g; Cholesterol: 175mg; Sodium: 620mg; Total Carbs: 25g; Dietary Fiber: 2g; Total Sugars: 1g; Protein: 33g

Turkey-hummus Wraps

Servings: 4 | Prep Time: 10 Minutes | Cooking Time: 7 Minutes Per Batch

Ingredients:

- 4 large whole wheat wraps
- ½ cup hummus
- 16 thin slices deli turkey
- 8 slices provolone cheese
- 1 cup fresh baby spinach (or more to taste)

Directions:

1. To assemble, place 2 tablespoons of hummus on each wrap and spread to within about 25 cm from edges. Top with 4 slices of turkey and 2 slices of provolone. Finish with 1/4 cup of baby spinach—or pile on as much as you like.
2. Roll up each wrap. You don't need to fold or seal the ends.
3. Place 2 wraps in air fryer basket, seam side down.
4. Cook at 180°C/360°F for 4 minutes to warm filling and melt cheese. If you like, you can continue cooking for 3 more minutes, until the wrap is slightly crispy.
5. Repeat step 4 to cook remaining wraps.

Variations & Ingredients Tips:

- Use flavored hummus like roasted red pepper or garlic.
- Add sliced cucumbers, tomatoes or roasted veggies.
- Make it vegetarian by using sliced feta or fresh mozzarella instead of turkey.

Per Serving: Calories: 420; Total Fat: 18g; Saturated Fat: 8g; Cholesterol: 55mg; Sodium: 1260mg; Total Carbs: 42g; Dietary Fiber: 5g; Total Sugars: 6g; Protein: 28g

Simple Salsa Chicken Thighs

Servings: 2 | Prep Time: 5 Minutes | Cooking Time: 35 Minutes

Ingredients:

- 454 grams boneless, skinless chicken thighs
- 1 cup mild chunky salsa
- ½ tsp taco seasoning
- 2 lime wedges for serving

Directions:

1. Preheat air fryer to 180°C/350°F.
2. Add chicken thighs into a baking pan and pour salsa and taco seasoning over.
3. Place the pan in the air fryer basket and Air Fry for 30 minutes until golden brown.
4. Serve with lime wedges.

Variations & Ingredients Tips:

- Use spicy salsa or add diced jalapeños for a kick of heat.
- Sprinkle with shredded cheddar cheese during the

last 5 minutes of cooking.
- Serve over rice, quinoa, or in tortillas for tacos.

Per Serving: Calories: 330; Total Fat: 11g; Saturated Fat: 3g; Sodium: 950mg; Total Carbohydrates: 10g; Dietary Fiber: 2g; Total Sugars: 6g; Protein: 45g

Chicken Nuggets

Servings: 20 | Prep Time: 20 Minutes | Cooking Time: 14 Minutes Per Batch

Ingredients:

- 450g boneless, skinless chicken thighs, cut into 2.5cm chunks
- 3/4 teaspoon salt
- 1/2 teaspoon black pepper
- 1/2 teaspoon garlic powder
- 1/2 teaspoon onion powder
- 1/2 cup flour
- 2 eggs, beaten
- 1/2 cup panko breadcrumbs
- 3 tablespoons plain breadcrumbs
- Oil for misting or cooking spray

Directions:

1. In a food processor, combine chicken, 1/2 tsp salt, pepper, garlic powder and onion powder. Pulse until finely chopped.
2. Place flour in one dish, beaten eggs in another. Mix panko, plain crumbs and 1/4 tsp salt in a third dish.
3. Shape chicken into nuggets. Dip in flour, egg, then crumb mixture.
4. Spray nuggets with oil and place in a single layer in air fryer basket.
5. Cook at 180°C/360°F for 10 mins. Spray with more oil and cook 4 more mins until golden.
6. Repeat step 5 for remaining batches.

Variations & Ingredients Tips:

- Use chicken breast meat instead of thighs.
- Add parmesan or ranch seasoning to the breadcrumb mix.
- Serve nuggets with honey mustard or barbecue sauce.

Per Serving (4 nuggets): Calories: 150; Total Fat: 5g; Saturated Fat: 1g; Cholesterol: 82mg; Sodium: 285mg; Total Carbs: 12g; Dietary Fiber: 1g; Total Sugars: 0g; Protein: 14g

Cheesy Chicken-avocado Paninis

Servings: 2 | Prep Time: 15 Minutes | Cooking Time: 25 Minutes

Ingredients:

- 2 tbsp mayonnaise
- 4 tsp yellow mustard
- 4 sandwich bread slices
- 113 grams sliced deli chicken ham
- 57 grams sliced provolone cheese
- 57 grams sliced mozzarella
- 1 avocado, sliced
- 1 tomato, sliced
- Salt and pepper to taste
- 1 tsp sesame seeds
- 2 tbsp butter, melted

Directions:

1. Preheat air fryer at 180°C/350°F.
2. Rub mayonnaise and mustard on the inside of each bread slice.
3. Top 2 bread slices with chicken ham, provolone and mozzarella cheese, avocado, sesame seeds, and tomato slices. Season with salt and pepper. Then, close sandwiches with the remaining bread slices.
4. Brush the top and bottom of each sandwich lightly with melted butter.
5. Place sandwiches in the air fryer basket and Bake for 6 minutes, flipping once.
6. Serve.

Variations & Ingredients Tips:

- Substitute chicken ham with sliced turkey, roast beef, or bacon.
- Use pesto, hummus, or guacamole instead of mayonnaise and mustard.
- Add sliced onions, bell peppers, or pickles for extra crunch and flavor.

Per Serving: Calories: 680; Total Fat: 49g; Saturated Fat: 20g; Sodium: 1460mg; Total Carbohydrates: 32g; Dietary Fiber: 6g; Total Sugars: 6g; Protein: 32g

Chicken Tenders With Basil-strawberry Glaze

Servings: 4 | Prep Time: 10 Minutes (plus 30 Minutes Marinating Time) | Cooking Time: 20 Minutes

Ingredients:

- 454 grams chicken tenderloins
- ¼ cup strawberry preserves
- 3 tbsp chopped basil
- 1 tsp orange juice
- ½ tsp orange zest
- Salt and pepper to taste

Directions:

1. Combine all ingredients, except for 1 tbsp of basil, in a bowl. Marinade in the fridge covered for 30 minutes.
2. Preheat air fryer to 180°C/350°F.
3. Place the chicken tenders in the air fryer basket and Air Fry for 4-6 minutes. Shake gently the basket and turn over the chicken. Cook for 5 more minutes.
4. Top with the remaining basil to serve.

Variations & Ingredients Tips:

- Use raspberry, apricot, or peach preserves instead of strawberry for different fruit flavors.
- Add a pinch of red pepper flakes or minced jalapeño to the marinade for a spicy kick.
- Serve over a bed of mixed greens or with a side of roasted veggies.

Per Serving: Calories: 250; Total Fat: 4g; Saturated Fat: 1g; Sodium: 200mg; Total Carbohydrates: 14g; Dietary Fiber: 0g; Total Sugars: 12g; Protein: 37g

Saucy Chicken Thighs

Servings: 4 | Prep Time: 10 Minutes | Cooking Time: 35 Minutes

Ingredients:

- 8 boneless, skinless chicken thighs
- 1 tbsp Italian seasoning
- Salt and pepper to taste
- 2 garlic cloves, minced
- ½ tsp apple cider vinegar
- ½ cup honey
- ¼ cup Dijon mustard

Directions:

1. Preheat air fryer to 200°C/400°F.
2. Season the chicken with Italian seasoning, salt, and black pepper. Place in the greased air fryer basket and Bake for 15 minutes, flipping once halfway through cooking.
3. While the chicken is cooking, add garlic, honey, vinegar, and Dijon mustard in a saucepan and stir-fry over medium heat for 4 minutes or until the sauce has thickened and warmed through.
4. Transfer the thighs to a serving dish and drizzle with honey-mustard sauce.
5. Serve and enjoy!

Variations & Ingredients Tips:

- Use bone-in, skin-on chicken thighs for crispier skin and juicier meat.
- Substitute Dijon mustard with grainy mustard or spicy brown mustard for a different flavor.
- Serve with roasted potatoes, green beans, or a side salad.

Per Serving: Calories: 400; Total Fat: 14g; Saturated Fat: 3.5g; Sodium: 550mg; Total Carbohydrates: 34g; Dietary Fiber: 0g; Total Sugars: 32g; Protein: 37g

Basic Chicken Breasts

Servings: 4 | Prep Time: 5 Minutes | Cooking Time: 15 Minutes

Ingredients:

- 2 tsp olive oil
- 2 chicken breasts
- Salt and pepper to taste
- ½ tsp garlic powder
- ½ tsp rosemary

Directions:

1. Preheat air fryer to 180°C/350°F.
2. Rub the chicken breasts with olive oil over tops and bottom and sprinkle with garlic powder, rosemary, salt, and pepper.
3. Place the chicken in the air fryer basket and Air Fry for 9 minutes, flipping once.
4. Let rest onto a serving plate for 5 minutes before cutting into cubes.
5. Serve and enjoy!

Variations & Ingredients Tips:

- Use boneless, skinless chicken thighs instead of breasts for juicier meat.
- Add a pinch of paprika, oregano, or thyme for extra herb flavor.
- Slice the chicken and serve over salads, pasta, or sandwiches.

Per Serving: Calories: 150; Total Fat: 6g; Saturated Fat:

1g; Sodium: 75mg; Total Carbohydrates: 0g; Dietary Fiber: 0g; Total Sugars: 0g; Protein: 24g

Christmas Chicken & Roasted Grape Salad

Servings: 4 | Prep Time: 20 Minutes | Cooking Time: 40 Minutes

Ingredients:

- 3 chicken breasts, pat-dried
- 1 tsp paprika
- Salt and pepper to taste
- 2 cups seedless red grapes
- ½ cup mayonnaise
- ½ cup plain yogurt
- 2 tbsp honey mustard
- 2 tbsp fresh lemon juice
- 1 cup chopped celery
- 2 scallions, chopped
- 2 tbsp walnuts, chopped

Directions:

1. Preheat the air fryer to 190°C/370°F.
2. Sprinkle the chicken breasts with paprika, salt, and pepper. Transfer to the greased air fryer basket and Air Fry for 16-19 minutes, flipping once. Remove and set on a cutting board.
3. Put the grapes in the fryer and spray with cooking oil. Fry for 4 minutes or until the grapes are hot and tender.
4. Mix the mayonnaise, yogurt, honey mustard, and lemon juice in a bowl and whisk.
5. Cube the chicken and add to the dressing along with the grapes, walnuts, celery, and scallions. Toss gently and serve.

Variations & Ingredients Tips:

- Use turkey, duck, or Cornish game hen instead of chicken for a festive twist.
- Substitute grapes with dried cranberries, cherries, or figs.
- Add chopped apples, pears, or persimmons for a fruity crunch.

Per Serving: Calories: 450; Total Fat: 29g; Saturated Fat: 5g; Sodium: 400mg; Total Carbohydrates: 20g; Dietary Fiber: 2g; Total Sugars: 15g; Protein: 32g

Cornish Hens With Honey-lime Glaze

Servings: 2 | Prep Time: 10 Minutes | Cooking Time: 30 Minutes

Ingredients:

- 1 Cornish game hen (680-907 grams)
- 1 tablespoon honey
- 1 tablespoon lime juice
- 1 teaspoon poultry seasoning
- salt and pepper
- cooking spray

Directions:

1. To split the hen into halves, cut through breast bone and down one side of the backbone.
2. Mix the honey, lime juice, and poultry seasoning together and brush or rub onto all sides of the hen. Season to taste with salt and pepper.
3. Spray air fryer basket with cooking spray and place hen halves in the basket, skin-side down.
4. Cook at 165°C/330°F for 30 minutes. Hen will be done when juices run clear when pierced at leg joint with a fork.
5. Let hen rest for 5 to 10 minutes before cutting.

Variations & Ingredients Tips:

- Use orange juice, soy sauce, or balsamic vinegar instead of lime juice for different glazes.
- Add minced garlic, ginger, or red pepper flakes to the glaze for extra flavor.
- Stuff the hen cavity with lemon wedges, garlic cloves, or fresh herbs before cooking.

Per Serving: Calories: 510; Total Fat: 28g; Saturated Fat: 8g; Sodium: 440mg; Total Carbohydrates: 11g; Dietary Fiber: 0g; Total Sugars: 10g; Protein: 54g

Fiery Chicken Meatballs

Servings: 4 | Prep Time: 15 Minutes | Cooking Time: 20 Minutes + Chilling Time

Ingredients:

- 2 jalapeños, seeded and diced
- 2 tbsp shredded Cheddar cheese
- 1 tsp Quick Pickled Jalapeños
- 2 tbsp white wine vinegar
- 1/2 tsp granulated sugar

- Salt and pepper to taste
- 1 tbsp ricotta cheese
- 340g ground chicken
- 1/4 tsp smoked paprika
- 1 tsp garlic powder
- 1 cup bread crumbs
- 1/4 tsp salt

Directions:

1. Combine the jalapeños, white wine vinegar, sugar, black pepper, and salt in a bowl. Let sit the jalapeño mixture in the fridge for 15 minutes.
2. In a bowl, combine ricotta cheese, cheddar cheese, and 1 tsp of the jalapeños. Form mixture into 8 balls.
3. Mix the ground chicken, smoked paprika, garlic powder, and salt in a bowl. Form mixture into 8 meatballs. Form a hole in the chicken meatballs, press a cheese ball into the hole and form chicken around the cheese ball, sealing the cheese ball in meatballs.
4. Preheat air fryer at 175°C/350°F. Mix the breadcrumbs and salt in a bowl. Roll stuffed meatballs in the mixture. Place the meatballs in the greased frying basket. Air Fry for 10 minutes, turning once.
5. Serve immediately.

Variations & Ingredients Tips:

▶ Use diced pickled jalapeños instead of fresh for a milder heat.
▶ Mix some chopped cilantro or parsley into the chicken.
▶ Serve with ranch or blue cheese dressing for dipping.

Per Serving: Calories: 270; Total Fat: 13g; Saturated Fat: 5g; Cholesterol: 115mg; Sodium: 610mg; Total Carbs: 14g; Dietary Fiber: 1g; Total Sugars: 2g; Protein: 24g

Gluten-free Nutty Chicken Fingers

Servings: 4 | Prep Time: 15 Minutes | Cooking Time: 10 Minutes

Ingredients:

- 1/2 cup gluten-free flour
- 1/2 teaspoon garlic powder
- 1/4 teaspoon onion powder
- 1/4 teaspoon black pepper
- 1/4 teaspoon salt
- 1 cup walnuts, pulsed into coarse flour
- 1/2 cup gluten-free breadcrumbs
- 2 large eggs
- 450g boneless, skinless chicken tenders

Directions:

1. Preheat the air fryer to 200°C/400°F.
2. In a medium bowl, mix the flour, garlic, onion, pepper, and salt. Set aside.
3. In a separate bowl, mix the walnut flour and breadcrumbs.
4. In a third bowl, whisk the eggs.
5. Liberally spray the air fryer basket with olive oil spray.
6. Pat the chicken tenders dry with a paper towel. Dredge the tenders one at a time in the flour, then dip them in the egg, and toss them in the breadcrumb coating. Repeat until all tenders are coated.
7. Set each tender in the air fryer, leaving room on each side of the tender to allow for flipping.
8. When the basket is full, cook 5 minutes, flip, and cook another 5 minutes. Check the internal temperature after cooking completes; it should read 74°C/165°F. If it does not, cook another 2 to 4 minutes.
9. Remove the tenders and let cool 5 minutes before serving. Repeat until all the tenders are cooked.

Variations & Ingredients Tips:

▶ Use pecans or almonds instead of walnuts.
▶ Add some dried herbs like thyme or oregano to the flour mix.
▶ Serve with honey mustard or BBQ sauce for dipping.

Per Serving: Calories: 380; Total Fat: 18g; Saturated Fat: 3g; Cholesterol: 170mg; Sodium: 360mg; Total Carbs: 19g; Dietary Fiber: 2g; Total Sugars: 2g; Protein: 37g

Chicken Wings Al Ajillo

Servings: 4 | Prep Time: 10 Minutes | Cooking Time: 35 Minutes

Ingredients:

- 907 grams chicken wings, split at the joint
- 2 tbsp melted butter
- 2 tbsp grated Cotija cheese
- 4 cloves garlic, minced
- ½ tbsp hot paprika
- ¼ tsp salt

Directions:

1. Preheat air fryer to 120°C/250°F.

2. Coat the chicken wings with 1 tbsp of butter. Place them in the basket and Air Fry for 12 minutes, tossing once.
3. In another bowl, whisk 1 tbsp of butter, Cotija cheese, garlic, hot paprika, and salt. Reserve.
4. Increase temperature to 200°C/400°F. Air Fry wings for 10 more minutes, tossing twice.
5. Transfer them to the bowl with the sauce, and toss to coat.
6. Serve immediately.

Variations & Ingredients Tips:

- Use drumettes or whole wings instead of split wings.
- Substitute Cotija cheese with Parmesan, Pecorino Romano, or feta.
- Add a dash of cayenne pepper or red pepper flakes for extra heat.

Per Serving: Calories: 510; Total Fat: 41g; Saturated Fat: 15g; Sodium: 580mg; Total Carbohydrates: 2g; Dietary Fiber: 0g; Total Sugars: 0g; Protein: 35g

Beef, Pork & Lamb Recipes

Greek Pita Pockets

Servings: 4 | Prep Time: 20 Minutes | Cooking Time: 7 Minutes

Ingredients:

- Dressing
- 1 cup plain yogurt
- 1 tbsp lemon juice
- 1 tsp dried dill weed, crushed
- 1 tsp ground oregano
- ½ tsp salt
- Meatballs
- 227 g ground lamb
- 1 tbsp diced onion
- 1 tsp dried parsley
- 1 tsp dried dill weed, crushed
- ¼ tsp oregano
- ¼ tsp coriander
- ¼ tsp ground cumin
- ¼ tsp salt
- 4 pita halves
- Suggested Toppings
- red onion, slivered
- seedless cucumber, thinly sliced
- crumbled Feta cheese
- sliced black olives
- chopped fresh peppers

Directions:

1. Stir dressing ingredients together and refrigerate while preparing lamb.
2. Combine all meatball ingredients in a large bowl and stir to distribute seasonings.
3. Shape meat mixture into 12 small meatballs, rounded or slightly flattened if you prefer.
4. Cook at 200°C/390°F for 7 minutes, until well done. Remove and drain on paper towels.
5. To serve, pile meatballs and your choice of toppings in pita pockets and drizzle with dressing.

Variations & Ingredients Tips:

- Try using ground beef, turkey or chicken instead of lamb
- Add some chopped spinach or kale to the meatball mixture for extra veggies
- Substitute tzatziki sauce for the yogurt dressing

Per Serving: Calories: 395; Total Fat: 19g; Saturated Fat: 8g; Cholesterol: 73mg; Sodium: 788mg; Total Carbs: 32g; Dietary Fiber: 1g; Total Sugars: 4g; Protein: 25g

Beef Fajitas

Servings: 2 | Prep Time: 5 Minutes | Cooking Time: 15 Minutes

Ingredients:

- 225 g sliced mushrooms
- ½ onion, cut into half-moons
- 1 tbsp olive oil
- Salt and pepper to taste
- 1 strip steak
- ½ tsp smoked paprika
- ½ tsp fajita seasoning
- 2 tbsp corn

Directions:

1. Preheat air fryer to 200°C/400°F. Combine the olive oil, onion, and salt in a bowl. Add the mushrooms and toss to coat. Spread in the frying basket. Sprinkle steak with salt, paprika, fajita seasoning and black pepper. Place steak on top of the mushroom mixture and air fry for 9 minutes, flipping steak once. Let rest onto a cutting board for 5 minutes before cutting in half. Divide steak, mushrooms, corn, and onions between 2 plates and serve.

Variations & Ingredients Tips:

- Add sliced bell peppers, jalapeños, or zucchini to the vegetable mixture for extra color and crunch.
- Use chicken, shrimp, or tofu instead of steak for different protein options.
- Serve with warm tortillas, rice, or beans for a complete fajita meal.

Per Serving: Calories: 331; Total Fat: 20g; Saturated Fat: 6g; Cholesterol: 74mg; Sodium: 172mg; Total Carbohydrates: 12g; Dietary Fiber: 2g; Total Sugars: 4g; Protein: 28g

Honey Pork Links

Servings: 4 | Prep Time: 10 Minutes | Cooking Time: 20 Minutes

Ingredients:

- 340 g ground mild pork sausage, removed from casings
- 1 tsp rubbed sage
- 2 tbsp honey
- ⅛ tsp cayenne pepper
- ⅛ tsp paprika
- Salt and pepper to taste

Directions:

1. Preheat air fryer to 200°C/400°F. Remove the sausage from the casings. Transfer to a bowl and add the remaining ingredients. Mix well. Make 8 links out of the mixture. Add the links to the frying basket and Air Fry for 8-10 minutes, flipping once. Serve right away.

Variations & Ingredients Tips:

- Use hot Italian sausage for a spicier kick
- Brush the links with BBQ sauce in the last few minutes of cooking
- Serve in hot dog buns with sautéed peppers and onions

Per Serving: Calories: 309; Total Fat: 23g; Saturated Fat: 8g; Cholesterol: 71mg; Sodium: 571mg; Total Carbs: 9g; Dietary Fiber: 0g; Total Sugars: 9g; Protein: 17g

Tuscan Veal Chops

Servings: 2 | Prep Time: 10 Minutes | Cooking Time: 12-15 Minutes

Ingredients:

- 4 teaspoons Olive oil
- 2 teaspoons Finely minced garlic
- 2 teaspoons Finely minced fresh rosemary leaves
- 1 teaspoon Finely grated lemon zest
- 1 teaspoon Crushed fennel seeds
- 1 teaspoon Table salt
- Up to 1/4 teaspoon Red pepper flakes
- 2 284g bone-in veal loin or rib chop(s), about 1.25cm thick

Directions:

1. Preheat the air fryer to 400°F/205°C.
2. Mix the oil, garlic, rosemary, lemon zest, fennel seeds, salt, and red pepper flakes in a small bowl. Rub this mixture onto both sides of the veal chop(s). Set aside at room temperature as the machine comes to temperature.
3. Set the chop(s) in the basket. If you're cooking more than one chop, leave as much air space between them as possible. Air-fry undisturbed for 12 minutes for medium-rare, or until an instant-read meat thermometer inserted into the center of a chop (without touching bone) registers 135°F/57°C (not USDA-approved). Or air-fry undisturbed for 15 minutes for medium-well, or until an instant-read meat thermometer registers 145°F/63°C (USDA-approved).
4. Use kitchen tongs to transfer the chops to a cutting board or a wire rack. Cool for 5 minutes before serving.

Variations & Ingredients Tips:

- Substitute dried herbs like oregano or thyme for the fresh rosemary
- Add grated parmesan to the herb coating for extra flavor
- Serve the chops with a lemon-caper sauce or red wine reduction

Per Serving: Calories: 370; Total Fat: 22g; Saturated Fat: 7g; Cholesterol: 190mg; Sodium: 730mg; Total Carbs: 2g; Dietary Fiber: 1g; Total Sugars: 0g; Protein: 39g

Beef Meatballs With Herbs

Servings: 6 | Prep Time: 10 Minutes | Cooking Time: 30 Minutes

Ingredients:

- 1 medium onion, minced
- 2 garlic cloves, minced
- 1 tsp olive oil
- 1 bread slice, crumbled
- 3 tbsp milk
- 1 tsp dried sage
- 1 tsp dried thyme
- 450 g ground beef

Directions:

1. Preheat air fryer to 190°C/380°F. Toss the onion, garlic, and olive oil in a baking pan, place it in the air fryer, and air fry for 2-4 minutes. The veggies should be crispy but tender. Transfer the veggies to a bowl and add in the breadcrumbs, milk, thyme, and sage, then toss gently to combine. Add in the ground beef and mix with your hands. Shape the mixture into 24 meatballs. Put them in the frying basket and air fry for 12-16 minutes or until the meatballs are browned on all sides. Serve and enjoy!

Variations & Ingredients Tips:

- Add grated Parmesan cheese, chopped parsley, or red pepper flakes to the meatball mixture for extra flavor.
- Serve with marinara sauce, pesto, or gravy for dipping or pouring over the meatballs.
- Use ground turkey, chicken, or pork instead of beef for leaner meatballs.

Per Serving: Calories: 187; Total Fat: 11g; Saturated Fat: 4g; Cholesterol: 62mg; Sodium: 86mg; Total Carbohydrates: 5g; Dietary Fiber: 1g; Total Sugars: 2g; Protein: 17g

Asy Carnitas

Servings: 3 | Prep Time: 10 Minutes (plus Marinating Time) | Cooking Time: 25 Minutes

Ingredients:

- 680 g boneless country-style pork ribs, cut into 5 cm pieces
- ¼ cup orange juice
- 2 tablespoons brine from a jar of pickles, any type, even pickled jalapeño rings (gluten-free, if a concern)
- 2 teaspoons minced garlic
- 2 teaspoons minced fresh oregano leaves
- ¾ teaspoon ground cumin
- ¾ teaspoon table salt
- ¾ teaspoon ground black pepper

Directions:

1. Mix the country-style pork rib pieces, orange juice, pickle brine, garlic, oregano, cumin, salt, and pepper in a large bowl. Cover and refrigerate for at least 2 hours or up to 10 hours, stirring the mixture occasionally.
2. Preheat the air fryer to 200°C/400°F. Set the rib pieces in their bowl on the counter as the machine heats.
3. Use kitchen tongs to transfer the rib pieces to the basket, arranging them in one layer. Some may touch. Air-fry for 25 minutes, turning and rearranging the pieces at the 10- and 20-minute marks to make sure all surfaces have been exposed to the air currents, until browned and sizzling.
4. Use clean kitchen tongs to transfer the rib pieces to a wire rack. Cool for a couple of minutes before serving.

Variations & Ingredients Tips:

- Use different types of citrus juice, such as lemon or lime, for a variety of flavors.
- Add some minced onion or jalapeño to the marinade for extra flavor.
- Serve the carnitas with warm tortillas, salsa, and guacamole for a classic Mexican meal.

Per Serving: Calories: 480; Total Fat: 30g; Saturated Fat: 10g; Cholesterol: 165mg; Sodium: 970mg; Total Carbs: 5g; Fiber: 0g; Sugars: 3g; Protein: 45g

Kentucky-style Pork Tenderloin

Servings: 2 | Prep Time: 10 Minutes | Cooking Time: 30 Minutes

Ingredients:

- 454g pork tenderloin, halved crosswise
- 1 tbsp smoked paprika
- 2 tsp ground cumin
- 1 tsp garlic powder
- 1 tsp shallot powder
- 1/4 tsp chili pepper
- Salt and pepper to taste
- 1 tsp Italian seasoning
- 2 tbsp butter, melted
- 1 tsp Worcestershire sauce

Directions:

1. Preheat air fryer to 350°F/177°C. In a shallow bowl, combine all spices. Set aside. In another bowl, whisk butter and Worcestershire sauce and brush over pork tenderloin. Sprinkle with the seasoning mix. Place pork in the lightly greased frying basket and Air Fry for 16 minutes, flipping once. Let sit onto a cutting board for 5 minutes before slicing. Serve immediately.

Variations & Ingredients Tips:

- Use smoked paprika or chipotle powder for a smoky flavor
- Add brown sugar or honey to the spice rub for a sweet-spicy glaze
- Brush tenderloin with mustard before applying rub for extra tang

Per Serving: Calories: 375; Total Fat: 16g; Saturated Fat: 7g; Cholesterol: 145mg; Sodium: 580mg; Total Carbs: 7g; Dietary Fiber: 2g; Total Sugars: 2g; Protein: 48g

Steak Fingers

Servings: 4 | Prep Time: 10 Minutes | Cooking Time: 8 Minutes

Ingredients:

- 4 small beef cube steaks
- salt and pepper
- ½ cup flour
- oil for misting or cooking spray

Directions:

1. Cut cube steaks into 2.5 cm-wide strips.
2. Sprinkle lightly with salt and pepper to taste.
3. Roll in flour to coat all sides.
4. Spray air fryer basket with cooking spray or oil.
5. Place steak strips in air fryer basket in single layer, very close together but not touching. Spray top of steak strips with oil or cooking spray.
6. Cook at 200°C/390°F for 4 minutes, turn strips over, and spray with oil or cooking spray.
7. Cook 4 more minutes and test with fork for doneness. Steak fingers should be crispy outside with no red juices inside. If needed, cook an additional 4 minutes or until well done. (Don't eat beef cube steak rare.)
8. Repeat steps 5 through 7 to cook remaining strips.

Variations & Ingredients Tips:

- Use seasoned breadcrumbs or cornmeal instead of flour for a crunchier coating
- Add some smoked paprika, garlic powder or cayenne to the flour for extra flavor
- Serve with ranch dressing, honey mustard or BBQ sauce for dipping

Per Serving: Calories: 292; Total Fat: 14g; Saturated Fat: 5g; Cholesterol: 77mg; Sodium: 105mg; Total Carbs: 13g; Dietary Fiber: 1g; Total Sugars: 0g; Protein: 30g

T-bone Steak With Roasted Tomato, Corn And Asparagus Salsa

Servings: 2 | Prep Time: 10 Minutes | Cooking Time: 15-20 Minutes

Ingredients:

- 1 (567g) T-bone steak
- Salt and freshly ground black pepper
- Salsa
- 1 1/2 cups cherry tomatoes
- 3/4 cup corn kernels (fresh, or frozen and thawed)
- 1 1/2 cups sliced asparagus (2.5cm slices) (about 1/2 bunch)
- 1 tablespoon + 1 teaspoon olive oil, divided
- Salt and freshly ground black pepper
- 1 1/2 teaspoons red wine vinegar
- 3 tablespoons chopped fresh basil
- 1 tablespoon chopped fresh chives

Directions:

1. Preheat the air fryer to 400°F/205°C.
2. Season the steak with salt and pepper and air-fry at 400°F/205°C for 10 minutes (medium-rare), 12 minutes (medium), or 15 minutes (well-done), flipping the steak once halfway through the cooking time.
3. In the meantime, toss the tomatoes, corn and aspara-

gus in a bowl with a teaspoon or so of olive oil, salt and freshly ground black pepper.
4. When the steak has finished cooking, remove it to a cutting board, tent loosely with foil and let it rest. Transfer the vegetables to the air fryer and air-fry at 400°F/205°C for 5 minutes, shaking the basket once or twice during the cooking process.
5. Transfer the cooked vegetables back into the bowl and toss with the red wine vinegar, remaining olive oil and fresh herbs.
6. To serve, slice the steak on the bias and serve with some of the salsa on top.

Variations & Ingredients Tips:

- Use different colored cherry tomatoes for a pop of color
- Substitute zucchini or bell peppers for the asparagus
- Add a squeeze of lemon juice to the salsa for extra brightness

Per Serving: Calories: 630; Total Fat: 32g; Saturated Fat: 10g; Cholesterol: 140mg; Sodium: 180mg; Total Carbs: 24g; Dietary Fiber: 5g; Total Sugars: 8g; Protein: 57g

Sage Pork With Potatoes

Servings: 4 | Prep Time: 15 Minutes | Cooking Time: 30 Minutes

Ingredients:

- 2 cups potatoes
- 2 teaspoons olive oil
- 454 g pork tenderloin, cubed
- 1 onion, chopped
- 1 red bell pepper, chopped
- 2 garlic cloves, minced
- ½ teaspoon dried sage
- ½ teaspoon fennel seeds, crushed
- 2 tablespoons chicken broth

Directions:

1. Preheat air fryer to 190°C/370°F. Add the potatoes and olive oil to a bowl and toss to coat. Transfer them to the frying basket and Air Fry for 15 minutes. Remove the bowl. Add the pork, onion, red bell pepper, garlic, sage, and fennel seeds, to the potatoes, add chicken broth and stir gently. Return the bowl to the frying basket and cook for 10 minutes. Be sure to shake the basket at least once. The pork should be cooked through and the potatoes soft and crispy. Serve immediately.

Variations & Ingredients Tips:

- Swap pork for chicken thighs or breasts cut into chunks
- Add some baby carrots or Brussels sprouts to the veggie mix
- Sprinkle with grated Parmesan before serving for cheesy flavor

Per Serving: Calories: 302; Total Fat: 8g; Saturated Fat: 2g; Cholesterol: 83mg; Sodium: 137mg; Total Carbs: 27g; Dietary Fiber: 3g; Total Sugars: 4g; Protein: 32g

Lamb Chops

Servings: 2 | Prep Time: 5 Minutes (plus Marinating Time) | Cooking Time: 20 Minutes

Ingredients:

- 2 teaspoons oil
- ½ teaspoon ground rosemary
- ½ teaspoon lemon juice
- 450 g lamb chops, approximately 2.5 cm thick
- Salt and pepper
- Cooking spray

Directions:

1. Mix the oil, rosemary, and lemon juice together and rub into all sides of the lamb chops. Season to taste with salt and pepper.
2. For best flavor, cover lamb chops and allow them to rest in the fridge for 20 minutes.
3. Spray air fryer basket with nonstick spray and place lamb chops in it.
4. Cook at 180°C/360°F for approximately 20 minutes. This will cook chops to medium. The meat will be juicy but have no remaining pink. Cook for a minute or two longer for well done chops. For rare chops, stop cooking after about 12 minutes and check for doneness.

Variations & Ingredients Tips:

- Use different herbs, such as thyme or oregano, for a variety of flavors.
- Add some minced garlic or Dijon mustard to the marinade for extra flavor.
- Serve the lamb chops with a side of roasted vegetables or mashed potatoes for a complete meal.

Per Serving: Calories: 450; Total Fat: 32g; Saturated Fat: 13g; Cholesterol: 145mg; Sodium: 130mg; Total Carbs: 0g; Fiber: 0g; Sugars: 0g; Protein: 38g

Apple Cornbread Stuffed Pork Loin With Apple Gravy

Servings: 4 | Prep Time: 20 Minutes | Cooking Time: 61 Minutes

Ingredients:

- 4 strips of bacon, chopped
- 1 Granny Smith apple, peeled, cored and finely chopped
- 2 teaspoons fresh thyme leaves
- ¼ cup chopped fresh parsley
- 2 cups cubed cornbread
- ½ cup chicken stock
- Salt and freshly ground black pepper
- 1 (900 g) boneless pork loin
- Kitchen twine
- Apple Gravy:
- 2 tablespoons butter
- 1 shallot, minced
- 1 Granny Smith apple, peeled, cored and finely chopped
- 3 sprigs fresh thyme
- 2 tablespoons flour
- 1 cup chicken stock
- ½ cup apple cider
- Salt and freshly ground black pepper, to taste

Directions:

1. Preheat the air fryer to 200°C/400°F.
2. Add the bacon to the air fryer and air-fry for 6 minutes until crispy. While the bacon is cooking, combine the apple, fresh thyme, parsley and cornbread in a bowl and toss well. Moisten the mixture with the chicken stock and season to taste with salt and freshly ground black pepper. Add the cooked bacon to the mixture.
3. Butterfly the pork loin by holding it flat on the cutting board with one hand, while slicing into the pork loin parallel to the cutting board with the other. Slice into the longest side of the pork loin, but stop before you cut all the way through. You should then be able to open the pork loin up like a book, making it twice as wide as it was when you started. Season the inside of the pork with salt and freshly ground black pepper.
4. Spread the cornbread mixture onto the butterflied pork loin, leaving a 2.5-cm border around the edge of the pork. Roll the pork loin up around the stuffing to enclose the stuffing, and tie the rolled pork in several places with kitchen twine or secure with toothpicks. Try to replace any stuffing that falls out of the roast as you roll it, by stuffing it into the ends of the rolled pork. Season the outside of the pork with salt and freshly ground black pepper.
5. Preheat the air fryer to 180°C/360°F.
6. Place the stuffed pork loin into the air fryer, seam side down. Air-fry the pork loin for 15 minutes at 180°C/360°F. Turn the pork loin over and air-fry for an additional 15 minutes. Turn the pork loin a quarter turn and air-fry for an additional 15 minutes. Turn the pork loin over again to expose the fourth side, and air-fry for an additional 10 minutes. The pork loin should register 70°C/155°F on an instant read thermometer when it is finished.
7. While the pork is cooking, make the apple gravy. Preheat a saucepan over medium heat on the stovetop and melt the butter. Add the shallot, apple and thyme sprigs and sauté until the apple starts to soften and brown a little. Add the flour and stir for a minute or two. Whisk in the stock and apple cider vigorously to prevent the flour from forming lumps. Bring the mixture to a boil to thicken and season to taste with salt and pepper.
8. Transfer the pork loin to a resting plate and loosely tent with foil, letting the pork rest for at least 5 minutes before slicing and serving with the apple gravy poured over the top.

Variations & Ingredients Tips:

▶ Use different types of bread, such as sourdough or whole wheat, for the stuffing for a variety of flavors and textures.
▶ Add some chopped nuts, such as pecans or walnuts, to the stuffing for a crunchy texture.
▶ Serve the pork loin with a side of roasted root vegetables or sautéed greens for a complete meal.

Per Serving: Calories: 690; Total Fat: 35g; Saturated Fat: 12g; Cholesterol: 180mg; Sodium: 780mg; Total Carbs: 37g; Fiber: 3g; Sugars: 15g; Protein: 58g

Taco Pie With Meatballs

Servings: 4 | Prep Time: 20 Minutes | Cooking Time: 40 Minutes + Cooling Time

Ingredients:

- 113 g shredded quesadilla cheese
- 113 g shredded Colby cheese
- 10 cooked meatballs, halved
- 237 g salsa
- 237 g canned refried beans
- 2 teaspoons chipotle powder

- ½ teaspoon ground cumin
- 4 corn tortillas

Directions:

1. Preheat the air fryer to 190°C/375°F. Combine the meatball halves, salsa, refried beans, chipotle powder, and cumin in a bowl. In a baking pan, add a tortilla and top with one-quarter of the meatball mixture. Sprinkle one-quarter of the cheeses on top and repeat the layers three more times, ending with cheese. Put the pan in the fryer. Bake for 15-20 minutes until the pie is bubbling and the cheese has melted. Let cool on a wire rack for 10 minutes. Run a knife around the edges of the pan and remove the sides of the pan, then cut into wedges to serve.

Variations & Ingredients Tips:

- Use ground beef, turkey or chorizo instead of meatballs
- Add layers of sliced jalapeños, olives or pickled onions
- Top with shredded lettuce, diced tomatoes and sour cream

Per Serving: Calories: 505; Total Fat: 27g; Saturated Fat: 14g; Cholesterol: 88mg; Sodium: 1228mg; Total Carbs: 38g; Dietary Fiber: 7g; Total Sugars: 5g; Protein: 29g

Crispy Lamb Shoulder Chops

Servings: 3 | Prep Time: 10 Minutes | Cooking Time: 28 Minutes

Ingredients:

- ¾ cup all-purpose flour or gluten-free all-purpose flour
- 2 teaspoons mild paprika
- 2 teaspoons table salt
- 1½ teaspoons garlic powder
- 1½ teaspoons dried sage leaves
- 3 lamb shoulder chops (170 g each), any excess fat trimmed
- Olive oil spray

Directions:

1. Whisk the flour, paprika, salt, garlic powder, and sage in a large bowl until the mixture is of a uniform color. Add the chops and toss well to coat. Transfer them to a cutting board.
2. Preheat the air fryer to 190°C/375°F.
3. When the machine is at temperature, again dredge the chops one by one in the flour mixture. Lightly coat both sides of each chop with olive oil spray before putting it in the basket. Continue on with the remaining chop(s), leaving air space between them in the basket.
4. Air-fry, turning once, for 25 minutes, or until the chops are well browned and tender when pierced with the point of a paring knife. If the machine is at 180°C/360°F, you may need to add up to 3 minutes to the cooking time.
5. Use kitchen tongs to transfer the chops to a wire rack. Cool for 5 minutes before serving.

Variations & Ingredients Tips:

- Use different types of seasoning, such as herbs de Provence or Italian seasoning, for a variety of flavors.
- Add some grated Parmesan cheese or nutritional yeast to the flour mixture for a cheesy flavor.
- Serve the lamb chops with a side of roasted vegetables or mashed potatoes for a complete meal.

Per Serving: Calories: 520; Total Fat: 30g; Saturated Fat: 11g; Cholesterol: 150mg; Sodium: 1560mg; Total Carbs: 22g; Fiber: 1g; Sugars: 0g; Protein: 41g

Wiener Schnitzel

Servings: 4 | Prep Time: 10 Minutes | Cooking Time: 14 Minutes

Ingredients:

- 4 thin boneless pork loin chops
- 2 tablespoons lemon juice
- 1/2 cup all-purpose flour
- 1 teaspoon salt
- 1/4 teaspoon marjoram
- 1 cup plain breadcrumbs
- 2 large eggs, beaten
- Oil for misting or cooking spray

Directions:

1. Rub the lemon juice into all sides of pork chops.
2. Mix together the flour, salt, and marjoram. Place flour mixture on a sheet of wax paper.
3. Place breadcrumbs on another sheet of wax paper.
4. Dip pork chops in flour, then beaten eggs, then breadcrumbs, coating both sides. Mist all sides with oil or cooking spray.
5. Spray air fryer basket with nonstick spray and place breaded pork chops in basket.

6. Cook at 198°C/390°F for 7 minutes. Turn chops, mist again with oil, and cook for another 7 minutes until well done.
7. Serve with lemon wedges.

Variations & Ingredients Tips:

- Use panko breadcrumbs instead of regular for extra crunch
- Add grated parmesan or lemon zest to the breadcrumb mixture
- Pound the pork chops thin if they are not thin-cut

Per Serving: Calories: 385; Total Fat: 10g; Saturated Fat: 2g; Cholesterol: 165mg; Sodium: 725mg; Total Carbs: 45g; Dietary Fiber: 1g; Total Sugars: 2g; Protein: 28g

Beef & Barley Stuffed Bell Peppers

Servings: 4 | Prep Time: 20 Minutes | Cooking Time: 30 Minutes

Ingredients:

- 1 cup pulled cooked roast beef
- 4 bell peppers, tops removed
- 1 onion, chopped
- ½ cup grated carrot
- 2 tsp olive oil
- 2 tomatoes, chopped
- 1 cup cooked barley
- 1 tsp dried marjoram

Directions:

1. Preheat air fryer to 200°C/400°F. Cut the tops of the bell peppers, then remove the stems. Put the onion, carrots, and olive oil in a baking pan and cook for 2-4 minutes. The veggies should be crispy but soft. Put the veggies in a bowl, toss in the tomatoes, barley, roast beef, and marjoram, and mix to combine. Spoon the veggie mix into the cleaned bell peppers and put them in the frying basket. Bake for 12-16 minutes or until the peppers are tender. Serve warm.

Variations & Ingredients Tips:

- Use ground beef, turkey, or sausage instead of roast beef for a different flavor.
- Add garlic, red pepper flakes, or smoked paprika to the filling for extra seasoning.
- Top with shredded cheese, sour cream, or chopped fresh herbs before serving.

Per Serving: Calories: 242; Total Fat: 8g; Saturated Fat: 2g; Cholesterol: 40mg; Sodium: 72mg; Total Carbohydrates: 27g; Dietary Fiber: 6g; Total Sugars: 8g; Protein: 17g

Indian Fry Bread Tacos

Servings: 4 | Prep Time: 15 Minutes | Cooking Time: 20 Minutes

Ingredients:

- 1 cup all-purpose flour
- 1½ tsp salt, divided
- 1½ tsp baking powder
- ¼ cup milk
- ¼ cup warm water
- 227 g lean ground beef
- One 410g can pinto beans, drained and rinsed
- 1 tbsp taco seasoning
- ½ cup shredded cheddar cheese
- 2 cups shredded lettuce
- ¼ cup black olives, chopped
- 1 Roma tomato, diced
- 1 avocado, diced
- 1 lime

Directions:

1. In a large bowl, whisk together the flour, 1 tsp of the salt, and baking powder. Make a well in the center and add in the milk and water. Form a ball and gently knead the dough four times. Cover the bowl with a damp towel, and set aside.
2. Preheat the air fryer to 190°C/380°F.
3. In a medium bowl, mix together the ground beef, beans, and taco seasoning. Crumble the meat mixture into the air fryer basket and cook for 5 minutes; toss the meat and cook an additional 2 to 3 minutes, or until cooked fully. Place the cooked meat in a bowl for taco assembly; season with the remaining ½ tsp salt as desired.
4. On a floured surface, place the dough. Cut the dough into 4 equal parts. Using a rolling pin, roll out each piece of dough to 12.5 cm in diameter. Spray the dough with cooking spray and place in the air fryer basket, working in batches as needed. Cook for 3 minutes, flip over, spray with cooking spray, and cook for an additional 1 to 3 minutes, until golden and puffy.
5. To assemble, place the fry breads on a serving platter. Equally divide the meat and bean mixture on top of the fry bread. Divide the cheese, lettuce, olives, tomatoes,

and avocado among the four tacos. Squeeze lime over the top prior to serving.

Variations & Ingredients Tips:

- Use ground turkey or shredded chicken instead of beef
- Add some sliced jalapeños or hot sauce for a spicy kick
- Offer sour cream, salsa and cilantro as additional toppings

Per Serving: Calories: 621; Total Fat: 28g; Saturated Fat: 9g; Cholesterol: 62mg; Sodium: 1472mg; Total Carbs: 64g; Dietary Fiber: 11g; Total Sugars: 3g; Protein: 30g

Mustard And Rosemary Pork Tenderloin With Fried Apples

Servings: 2 | Prep Time: 10 Minutes | Cooking Time: 26 Minutes

Ingredients:

- 1 pork tenderloin (about 450 g)
- 2 tablespoons coarse brown mustard
- Salt and freshly ground black pepper
- 1½ teaspoons finely chopped fresh rosemary, plus sprigs for garnish
- 2 apples, cored and cut into 8 wedges
- 1 tablespoon butter, melted
- 1 teaspoon brown sugar

Directions:

1. Preheat the air fryer to 190°C/370°F.
2. Cut the pork tenderloin in half so that you have two pieces that fit into the air fryer basket. Brush the mustard onto both halves of the pork tenderloin and then season with salt, pepper and the fresh rosemary. Place the pork tenderloin halves into the air fryer basket and air-fry for 10 minutes. Turn the pork over and air-fry for an additional 8 minutes or until the internal temperature of the pork registers 70°C/155°F on an instant read thermometer. If your pork tenderloin is especially thick, you may need to add a minute or two, but it's better to check the pork and add time, than to overcook it.
3. Let the pork rest for 5 minutes. In the meantime, toss the apple wedges with the butter and brown sugar and air-fry at 200°C/400°F for 8 minutes, shaking the basket once or twice during the cooking process so the apples cook and brown evenly.
4. Slice the pork on the bias. Serve with the fried apples scattered over the top and a few sprigs of rosemary as garnish.

Variations & Ingredients Tips:

- Use different types of mustard, such as Dijon or whole grain, for a variety of flavors.
- Add some minced garlic or shallots to the pork tenderloin for extra flavor.
- Serve the pork and apples with a side of roasted potatoes or sautéed green beans for a complete meal.

Per Serving: Calories: 380; Total Fat: 14g; Saturated Fat: 6g; Cholesterol: 135mg; Sodium: 410mg; Total Carbs: 21g; Fiber: 4g; Sugars: 15g; Protein: 44g

Beef & Spinach Sautée

Servings: 4 | Prep Time: 10 Minutes | Cooking Time: 30 Minutes

Ingredients:

- 2 tomatoes, chopped
- 2 tbsp crumbled goat cheese
- 225 g ground beef
- 1 shallot, chopped
- 2 garlic cloves, minced
- 2 cups baby spinach
- 2 tbsp lemon juice
- 80 ml beef broth

Directions:

1. Preheat air fryer to 190°C/370°F. Crumble the beef in a baking pan and place it in the air fryer. Air fry for 3-7 minutes, stirring once. Drain the meat and make sure it's browned. Toss in the tomatoes, shallot, and garlic and air fry for an additional 4-8 minutes until soft. Toss in the spinach, lemon juice, and beef broth and cook for 2-4 minutes until the spinach wilts. Top with goat cheese and serve.

Variations & Ingredients Tips:

- Use ground turkey, chicken, or pork instead of beef for a leaner option.
- Add sliced mushrooms, bell peppers, or zucchini for extra veggies.
- Serve over rice, quinoa, or pasta for a heartier meal.

Per Serving: Calories: 215; Total Fat: 13g; Saturated Fat: 6g; Cholesterol: 56mg; Sodium: 253mg; Total Carbohydrates: 6g; Dietary Fiber: 2g; Total Sugars: 3g; Protein:

17g

Greek-style Pork Stuffed Jalapeño Poppers

Servings: 6 | Prep Time: 20 Minutes | Cooking Time: 30 Minutes

Ingredients:

- 6 jalapeños, halved lengthwise
- 3 tbsp diced Kalamata olives
- 3 tbsp olive oil
- 113g ground pork
- 2 tbsp feta cheese
- 28g cream cheese, softened
- ½ tsp dried mint
- ½ cup Greek yogurt

Directions:

1. Warm 2 tbsp of olive oil in a skillet over medium heat. Stir in ground pork and cook for 6 minutes until no longer pink. Preheat air fryer to 175°C/350°F. Mix the cooked pork, olives, feta cheese, and cream cheese in a bowl. Divide the pork mixture between the peppers. Place them in the frying basket and Air Fry for 6 minutes. Mix the Greek yogurt with the remaining olive oil and mint in a small bowl. Serve with the poppers.

Variations & Ingredients Tips:

- Use stuffed banana peppers or mini bell peppers for a milder option
- Mix some chopped spinach or sun-dried tomatoes into the filling
- Drizzle with balsamic glaze before serving for a sweet and tangy finish

Per Serving: Calories: 207; Total Fat: 18g; Saturated Fat: 6g; Cholesterol: 34mg; Sodium: 347mg; Total Carbs: 3g; Dietary Fiber: 1g; Total Sugars: 2g; Protein: 8g

Fish And Seafood Recipes

Lobster Tails With Lemon Garlic Butter

Servings: 2 | Prep Time: 10 Minutes | Cooking Time: 5 Minutes

Ingredients:

- 115-g unsalted butter
- 1 tablespoon finely chopped lemon zest
- 1 clove garlic, thinly sliced
- 2 (170-g) lobster tails
- Salt and freshly ground black pepper
- 1/2 cup white wine
- 1/2 lemon, sliced
- Vegetable oil

Directions:

1. Make the lemon garlic butter by combining butter, lemon zest and garlic in a saucepan. Melt and simmer over low heat while preparing the lobster.
2. Cut down the top shell of each lobster tail. Crack the bottom shell so you can access the meat inside. Pull meat up out of shell, leaving it attached at the base.
3. Lay meat over shell and season with salt and pepper. Pour some lemon garlic butter over meat and refrigerate briefly to solidify butter.
4. Pour white wine into air fryer drawer and add lemon slices. Preheat to 200°C/400°F for 5 mins.
5. Transfer lobsters to air fryer basket. Air-fry at 190°C/370°F for 5 mins, brushing more butter on halfway through. (Add 1-2 mins if tails are over 170-g.)
6. Serve with remaining butter for dipping.

Variations & Ingredients Tips:

- Add dried herbs like thyme or parsley to the butter.
- Stuff the tail cavity with breadcrumbs before cooking.

- Squeeze lemon juice over lobster before serving.

Per Serving: Calories: 550; Total Fat: 45g; Saturated Fat: 28g; Cholesterol: 140mg; Sodium: 600mg; Total Carbs: 6g; Dietary Fiber: 0g; Total Sugars: 1g; Protein: 22g

Better Fish Sticks

Servings: 3 | Prep Time: 10 Minutes | Cooking Time: 8 Minutes

Ingredients:

- ¾ cup Seasoned Italian-style dried bread crumbs (gluten-free, if a concern)
- 3 tablespoons (about 15g) finely grated Parmesan cheese
- 280g skinless cod fillets, cut lengthwise into 2.5-cm-wide pieces
- 3 tablespoons regular or low-fat mayonnaise (not fat-free; gluten-free, if a concern)
- Vegetable oil spray

Directions:

1. Preheat the air fryer to 200°C/400°F.
2. Mix the bread crumbs and grated Parmesan in a shallow soup bowl or a small pie plate.
3. Smear the fish fillet sticks completely with the mayonnaise, then dip them one by one in the bread-crumb mixture, turning and pressing gently to make an even and thorough coating. Coat each stick on all sides with vegetable oil spray.
4. Set the fish sticks in the basket with at least 6 mm between them. Air-fry undisturbed for 8 minutes, or until golden brown and crisp.
5. Use a nonstick-safe spatula to gently transfer them from the basket to a wire rack. Cool for only a minute or two before serving.

Variations & Ingredients Tips:

- Use salmon, tilapia or haddock instead of cod.
- Add some garlic powder, paprika or Old Bay seasoning to the breading mix.
- Serve with tartar sauce, ketchup or honey mustard for dipping.

Per Serving: Calories: 270; Total Fat: 12g; Saturated Fat: 2.5g; Cholesterol: 70mg; Sodium: 620mg; Total Carbs: 18g; Dietary Fiber: 1g; Total Sugars: 2g; Protein: 23g

Fish Sticks With Tartar Sauce

Servings: 2 | Prep Time: 15 Minutes | Cooking Time: 6 Minutes

Ingredients:

- 340g cod or flounder
- 1/2 cup flour
- 1/2 teaspoon paprika
- 1 teaspoon salt
- Freshly ground black pepper
- 2 eggs, lightly beaten
- 1 1/2 cups panko breadcrumbs
- 1 teaspoon salt
- Vegetable oil
- Tartar Sauce:
- 1/4 cup mayonnaise
- 2 teaspoons lemon juice
- 2 tablespoons finely chopped sweet pickles
- Salt and pepper

Directions:

1. Cut fish into 2cm wide sticks. Set up 3 dishes: flour+spices, eggs, and breadcrumbs+salt.
2. Coat fish in flour, egg, then breadcrumbs, pressing to adhere.
3. Preheat air fryer to 200°C/400°F. Spray fish with oil.
4. Air fry for 4 mins, flip and cook 2 more mins.
5. Make tartar sauce by mixing ingredients.
6. Serve fish sticks warm with tartar sauce.

Variations & Ingredients Tips:

- Add Old Bay or cajun seasoning to the breadcrumb mix.
- Bake instead of air frying at 400°F for 12-15 mins.
- Serve with lemon wedges, malt vinegar or rémoulade sauce.

Per Serving: Calories: 469; Total Fat: 17g; Saturated Fat: 3g; Cholesterol: 202mg; Sodium: 1710mg; Total Carbs: 48g; Dietary Fiber: 2g; Total Sugars: 2g; Protein: 30g

Beer-battered Cod

Servings: 3 | Prep Time: 15 Minutes | Cooking Time: 12 Minutes

Ingredients:

- 1½ cups All-purpose flour
- 3 tablespoons Old Bay seasoning

- 1 large egg
- ¼ cup Amber beer, pale ale, or IPA
- 3 (115g) skinless cod fillets
- Vegetable oil spray

Directions:

1. Preheat the air fryer to 200°C/400°F.
2. Set up and fill two shallow soup plates or small pie plates on your counter: one with the flour, whisked with the Old Bay until well combined; and one with the egg, whisked with the beer until foamy and uniform.
3. Dip a piece of cod in the flour mixture, turning it to coat on all sides (not just the top and bottom). Gently shake off any excess flour and dip the fish in the egg mixture, turning it to coat. Let any excess egg mixture slip back into the rest, then set the fish back in the flour mixture and coat it again, then back in the egg mixture for a second wash, then back in the flour mixture for a third time. Coat the fish on all sides with vegetable oil spray and set it aside. "Batter" the remaining piece(s) of cod in the same way.
4. Set the coated cod fillets in the basket with as much space between them as possible. They should not touch. Air-fry undisturbed for 12 minutes, or until brown and crisp.
5. Use kitchen tongs to gently transfer the fish to a wire rack. Cool for only a couple of minutes before serving.

Variations & Ingredients Tips:

- Use haddock, pollack or catfish instead of cod.
- Substitute beer with sparkling water for a non-alcoholic version.
- Serve with french fries, coleslaw and malt vinegar.

Per Serving: Calories: 330; Total Fat: 5g; Saturated Fat: 1g; Cholesterol: 115mg; Sodium: 1120mg; Total Carbs: 44g; Dietary Fiber: 2g; Total Sugars: 1g; Protein: 26g

Caribbean Jerk Cod Fillets

Servings: 2 | Prep Time: 10 Minutes | Cooking Time: 20 Minutes

Ingredients:

- ¼ cup chopped cooked shrimp
- ¼ cup diced mango
- 1 tomato, diced
- 2 tbsp diced red onion
- 1 tbsp chopped parsley
- ¼ tsp ginger powder
- 2 tsp lime juice
- Salt and pepper to taste
- 2 cod fillets
- 2 tsp Jerk seasoning

Directions:

1. In a bowl, combine the shrimp, mango, tomato, red onion, parsley, ginger powder, lime juice, salt, and black pepper. Let chill the salsa in the fridge until ready to use.
2. Preheat air fryer to 180°C/350°F.
3. Sprinkle cod fillets with Jerk seasoning. Place them in the greased air fryer basket and Air Fry for 10 minutes or until the cod is opaque and flakes easily with a fork.
4. Divide between 2 medium plates. Serve topped with the Caribbean salsa.

Variations & Ingredients Tips:

- Substitute cod with halibut, mahi-mahi, or snapper fillets.
- Use pineapple or papaya instead of mango for a different tropical flavor.
- Add a dash of hot sauce or minced jalapeño to the salsa for extra heat.

Per Serving: Calories: 200; Total Fat: 2g; Saturated Fat: 0g; Sodium: 530mg; Total Carbohydrates: 14g; Dietary Fiber: 2g; Total Sugars: 9g; Protein: 32g

Fish Cakes

Servings: 4 | Prep Time: 20 Minutes | Cooking Time: 10 Minutes

Ingredients:

- 3/4 cup mashed potatoes (about 1 large russet potato)
- 340g cod or other white fish
- Salt and pepper
- Oil for misting or cooking spray
- 1 large egg
- 1/4 cup potato starch
- 1/2 cup panko breadcrumbs
- 1 tablespoon fresh chopped chives
- 2 tablespoons minced onion

Directions:

1. Peel potatoes, cut into cubes, and cook on stovetop till soft.
2. Salt and pepper raw fish to taste. Mist with oil or cook-

ing spray, and cook in air fryer at 180°C/360°F for 6 to 8 minutes, until fish flakes easily. If fish is crowded, rearrange halfway through cooking to ensure all pieces cook evenly.
3. Transfer fish to a plate and break apart to cool.
4. Beat egg in a shallow dish.
5. Place potato starch in another shallow dish, and panko crumbs in a third dish.
6. When potatoes are done, drain in colander and rinse with cold water.
7. In a large bowl, mash the potatoes and stir in the chives and onion. Add salt and pepper to taste, then stir in the fish.
8. If needed, stir in a tablespoon of the beaten egg to help bind the mixture.
9. Shape into 8 small, fat patties. Dust lightly with potato starch, dip in egg, and roll in panko crumbs. Spray both sides with oil or cooking spray.
10. Cook at 180°C/360°F for 10 minutes, until golden brown and crispy.

Variations & Ingredients Tips:

- Add some lemon zest, capers or dill to the fish cake mixture.
- Use sweet potatoes instead of white for a different flavor.
- Serve with tartar sauce, aioli or malt vinegar.

Per Serving: Calories: 240; Total Fat: 4g; Saturated Fat: 1g; Cholesterol: 95mg; Sodium: 230mg; Total Carbs: 28g; Dietary Fiber: 1g; Total Sugars: 1g; Protein: 22g

Aromatic Ahi Tuna Steaks

Servings: 4 | Prep Time: 5 Minutes | Cooking Time: 15 Minutes

Ingredients:

- 1 tsp garlic powder
- 1/2 tsp salt
- 1/4 tsp dried thyme
- 1/4 tsp dried oregano
- 1/4 tsp cayenne pepper
- 4 ahi tuna steaks
- 2 tbsp olive oil
- 1 lemon, cut into wedges

Directions:

1. Preheat air fryer to 190°C/380°F.
2. Stir together the garlic powder, salt, thyme, cayenne pepper and oregano in a bowl to combine.
3. Coat the tuna steaks with olive oil. Season both sides of each steak with the seasoning mix.
4. Put the steaks in the frying basket. Air Fry for 5 minutes, then flip and cook for an additional 3-4 minutes.
5. Serve warm with lemon wedges on the side.

Variations & Ingredients Tips:

- Use salmon, swordfish or mahi mahi instead of tuna.
- Add a sprinkle of sesame seeds before air frying.
- Serve over a bed of salad greens or rice.

Per Serving: Calories: 220; Total Fat: 8g; Saturated Fat: 1.5g; Cholesterol: 65mg; Sodium: 380mg; Total Carbs: 1g; Dietary Fiber: 0g; Total Sugars: 0g; Protein: 34g

Smoked Paprika Cod Goujons

Servings: 2 | Prep Time: 10 Minutes | Cooking Time: 30 Minutes

Ingredients:

- 1 (225g) cod fillet, cut into chunks
- 2 eggs, beaten
- 1/4 cup breadcrumbs
- 1/4 cup rice flour
- 1 lemon, juiced
- 1/2 tbsp garlic powder
- 1 tsp smoked paprika
- Salt and pepper to taste

Directions:

1. Preheat air fryer to 175°C/350°F.
2. In a bowl, mix beaten eggs and lemon juice.
3. Dip cod chunks in the egg mixture.
4. In another bowl, mix breadcrumbs, rice flour, garlic, smoked paprika, salt & pepper.
5. Coat cod in the crumb mixture.
6. Transfer coated cod to greased air fryer basket.
7. Air Fry for 14-16 minutes until golden brown and cooked through, tossing a few times.
8. Serve.

Variations & Ingredients Tips:

- Use regular or panko breadcrumbs instead of rice flour.
- Add cayenne pepper or paprika to the crumb mixture for extra heat.
- Serve with lemon wedges and tartar sauce for dipping.

Per Serving: Calories: 270; Total Fat: 5g; Saturated Fat: 1g; Cholesterol: 190mg; Sodium: 400mg; Total Carbs: 27g; Dietary Fiber: 1g; Sugars: 2g; Protein: 28g

Crunchy Clam Strips

Servings: 3 | Prep Time: 10 Minutes | Cooking Time: 8 Minutes

Ingredients:

- 225g Clam strips, drained
- 1 Large egg, well beaten
- 1/2 cup All-purpose flour
- 1/2 cup Yellow cornmeal
- 1 1/2 teaspoons Table salt
- 1 1/2 teaspoons Ground black pepper
- Up to 3/4 teaspoon Cayenne
- Vegetable oil spray

Directions:

1. Preheat the air fryer to 200°C/400°F.
2. Toss the clam strips and beaten egg in a bowl until the clams are well coated.
3. Mix the flour, cornmeal, salt, pepper, and cayenne in a large zip-closed plastic bag until well combined.
4. Using a fork or tongs, transfer clam strips from egg to flour bag. Seal and shake to coat.
5. Remove strips from bag, leaving excess flour mixture behind. Coat strips with oil spray.
6. Spread strips in air fryer basket in one layer. Air fry for 8 minutes until browned and crunchy.
7. Transfer cooked strips to a serving platter. Let cool briefly before serving hot.

Variations & Ingredients Tips:

- Use Old Bay seasoning or cajun seasoning instead of cayenne.
- Substitute Panko breadcrumbs for some of the flour coating.
- Serve with lemon wedges and tartar sauce or cocktail sauce.

Per Serving: Calories: 208; Total Fat: 4g; Saturated Fat: 1g; Cholesterol: 146mg; Sodium: 896mg; Total Carbs: 29g; Dietary Fiber: 1g; Total Sugars: 0g; Protein: 14g

Fish Tortillas With Coleslaw

Servings: 4 | Prep Time: 15 Minutes | Cooking Time: 30 Minutes

Ingredients:

- 1 tbsp olive oil
- 450g cod fillets
- 3 tbsp lemon juice
- 2 cups chopped red cabbage
- 1/2 cup salsa
- 1/3 cup sour cream
- 6 taco shells, warm
- 1 avocado, chopped

Directions:

1. Preheat air fryer to 200°C/400°F.
2. Brush oil on the cod and sprinkle with some lemon juice. Place in the frying basket and Air Fry until the fish flakes with a fork, 9-12 minutes.
3. Meanwhile, mix together the remaining lemon juice, red cabbage, salsa, and sour cream in a medium bowl.
4. Put the cooked fish in a bowl, breaking it into large pieces. Then add the cabbage mixture, avocados, and warmed tortilla shells ready for assembly.
5. Enjoy!

Variations & Ingredients Tips:

- Use tilapia, mahi mahi or catfish instead of cod.
- Add some chopped jalapeños or hot sauce to the slaw for a kick.
- Serve with lime wedges, cilantro and sliced radishes.

Per Serving: Calories: 370; Total Fat: 19g; Saturated Fat: 5g; Cholesterol: 75mg; Sodium: 620mg; Total Carbs: 27g; Dietary Fiber: 5g; Total Sugars: 4g; Protein: 29g

Basil Mushroom & Shrimp Spaghetti

Servings: 6 | Prep Time: 10 Minutes | Cooking Time: 20 Minutes

Ingredients:

- 225g baby Bella mushrooms, sliced
- 1/2 cup grated Parmesan
- 450g peeled shrimp, deveined
- 3 tbsp olive oil
- 1/4 tsp garlic powder
- 1/4 tsp shallot powder
- 1/4 tsp cayenne
- 450g cooked pasta spaghetti
- 5 garlic cloves, minced
- Salt and pepper to taste

- 1/2 cup dill

Directions:

1. Preheat air fryer to 190°C/380°F.
2. Toss the shrimp, 1 tbsp of olive oil, garlic powder, shallot powder and cayenne in a bowl. Put the shrimp into the frying basket and Roast for 5 minutes. Remove and set aside.
3. Warm the remaining olive oil in a large skillet over medium heat. Add the garlic and mushrooms and cook for 5 minutes.
4. Pour in the pasta, 1/2 cup of water, Parmesan, salt, pepper, and dill and stir to coat the pasta. Stir in the shrimp.
5. Remove from heat, then let the mixture rest for 5 minutes. Serve and enjoy!

Variations & Ingredients Tips:

- Use linguine, fettuccine or angel hair pasta instead of spaghetti.
- Add some halved cherry tomatoes or baby spinach leaves.
- Sprinkle with red pepper flakes for a kick of heat.

Per Serving: Calories: 390; Total Fat: 13g; Saturated Fat: 3.5g; Cholesterol: 145mg; Sodium: 440mg; Total Carbs: 43g; Dietary Fiber: 2g; Total Sugars: 2g; Protein: 28g

Cilantro Sea Bass

Servings: 2 | Prep Time: 5 Minutes | Cooking Time: 15 Minutes

Ingredients:

- Salt and pepper to taste
- 1 tsp olive oil
- 2 sea bass fillets
- 1/2 tsp berbere seasoning
- 2 tsp chopped cilantro
- 1 tsp dried thyme
- 1/2 tsp garlic powder
- 4 lemon quarters

Directions:

1. Preheat air fryer at 190°C/375°F.
2. Rub sea bass fillets with olive oil, thyme, garlic powder, salt and black pepper. Season with berbere seasoning.
3. Place fillets in the greased frying basket and Air Fry for 6-8 minutes. Let rest for 5 minutes on a serving plate.
4. Scatter with cilantro and serve with lemon quarters on the side.

Variations & Ingredients Tips:

- Use cod, halibut or snapper instead of sea bass.
- Add a sprinkle of smoked paprika or cayenne for heat.
- Serve over a bed of cilantro-lime rice or quinoa.

Per Serving: Calories: 220; Total Fat: 8g; Saturated Fat: 1.5g; Cholesterol: 70mg; Sodium: 200mg; Total Carbs: 2g; Dietary Fiber: 1g; Total Sugars: 0g; Protein: 34g

Crab Cakes

Servings: 2 | Prep Time: 20 Minutes | Cooking Time: 10 Minutes

Ingredients:

- 1 teaspoon butter
- 1/3 cup finely diced onion
- 1/3 cup finely diced celery
- 1/4 cup mayonnaise
- 1 teaspoon Dijon mustard
- 1 egg
- Pinch ground cayenne pepper
- 1 teaspoon salt
- Freshly ground black pepper
- 450g lump crabmeat
- 1/2 cup + 2 tablespoons panko breadcrumbs, divided

Directions:

1. Melt the butter in a skillet over medium heat. Sauté the onion and celery until it starts to soften, but not brown – about 4 minutes. Transfer the cooked vegetables to a large bowl.
2. Add the mayonnaise, Dijon mustard, egg, cayenne pepper, salt and freshly ground black pepper to the bowl. Gently fold in the lump crabmeat and 2 tablespoons of panko breadcrumbs. Stir carefully so you don't break up all the crab pieces.
3. Preheat the air fryer to 200°C/400°F.
4. Place the remaining panko breadcrumbs in a shallow dish. Divide the crab mixture into 4 portions and shape each portion into a round patty. Dredge the crab patties in the breadcrumbs, coating both sides as well as the edges with the crumbs.
5. Air-fry the crab cakes for 5 minutes. Using a flat spatula, gently turn the cakes over and air-fry for another 5 minutes. Serve the crab cakes with tartar sauce or

cocktail sauce, or dress it up with the suggestion below.

Variations & Ingredients Tips:

- Add some Old Bay seasoning or Cajun spice to the mix.
- Form into mini crab cakes and serve as an appetizer.
- Top with a lemon-herb aioli or spicy remoulade.

Per Serving: Calories: 420; Total Fat: 24g; Saturated Fat: 5g; Cholesterol: 275mg; Sodium: 1720mg; Total Carbs: 21g; Dietary Fiber: 1g; Total Sugars: 3g; Protein: 32g

Halibut With Coleslaw

Servings: 4 | Prep Time: 15 Minutes | Cooking Time: 30 Minutes

Ingredients:

- 1 bag coleslaw mix
- 1/4 cup mayonnaise
- 1 tsp lemon zest
- 1 tbsp lemon juice
- 1 shredded carrot
- 1/2 cup buttermilk
- 1 tsp grated onion
- 4 halibut fillets
- Salt and pepper to taste

Directions:

1. Combine coleslaw mix, mayonnaise, carrot, buttermilk, onion, lemon zest, lemon juice, and salt in a bowl. Let chill the coleslaw covered in the fridge until ready to use.
2. Preheat air fryer at 175°C/350°F.
3. Sprinkle halibut with salt and pepper. Place them in the greased frying basket and Air Fry for 10 minutes until the fillets are opaque and flake easily with a fork.
4. Serve with chilled coleslaw.

Variations & Ingredients Tips:

- Add some chopped apples, raisins or pineapple to the coleslaw.
- Use Greek yogurt instead of mayo for a lighter dressing.
- Serve the fish and slaw in tacos, wraps or sliders.

Per Serving: Calories: 290; Total Fat: 10g; Saturated Fat: 2.5g; Cholesterol: 100mg; Sodium: 460mg; Total Carbs: 13g; Dietary Fiber: 2g; Total Sugars: 6g; Protein: 36g

Quick Tuna Tacos

Servings: 4 | Prep Time: 15 Minutes | Cooking Time: 20 Minutes

Ingredients:

- 2 cups torn romaine lettuce
- 450g fresh tuna steak, cubed
- 1 tbsp grated fresh ginger
- 2 garlic cloves, minced
- 1/2 tsp toasted sesame oil
- 4 tortillas
- 1/4 cup mild salsa
- 1 red bell pepper, sliced

Directions:

1. Preheat air fryer to 200°C/390°F.
2. Combine the tuna, ginger, garlic, and sesame oil in a bowl and allow to marinate for 10 minutes.
3. Lay the marinated tuna in the fryer and Grill for 4-7 minutes.
4. Serve right away with tortillas, mild salsa, lettuce, and bell pepper for delicious tacos.

Variations & Ingredients Tips:

- Use corn or flour tortillas.
- Top with avocado, sour cream or shredded cabbage.
- Marinate the tuna longer for more flavor.

Per Serving: Calories: 270; Total Fat: 6g; Saturated Fat: 1g; Cholesterol: 55mg; Sodium: 440mg; Total Carbs: 23g; Dietary Fiber: 2g; Sugars: 2g; Protein: 31g

Classic Crab Cakes

Servings: 4 | Prep Time: 15 Minutes | Cooking Time: 10 Minutes

Ingredients:

- 280g lump crabmeat, picked over for shell and cartilage
- 6 tablespoons plain panko bread crumbs (gluten-free, if a concern)
- 6 tablespoons chopped drained jarred roasted red peppers
- 4 medium scallions, trimmed and thinly sliced
- 1/4 cup regular or low-fat mayonnaise (not fat-free; gluten-free, if a concern)
- 1/4 teaspoon dried dill

- 1/4 teaspoon dried thyme
- 1/4 teaspoon onion powder
- 1/4 teaspoon table salt
- 1/8 teaspoon celery seeds
- Up to 1/8 teaspoon cayenne
- Vegetable oil spray

Directions:

1. Preheat the air fryer to 200°C/400°F.
2. Gently mix the crabmeat, bread crumbs, red pepper, scallion, mayonnaise, dill, thyme, onion powder, salt, celery seeds, and cayenne in a bowl until well combined.
3. Use clean and dry hands to form 1/2 cup of this mixture into a tightly packed 2.5-cm-thick, 7.5- to 10-cm-wide patty. Coat the top and bottom of the patty with vegetable oil spray and set it aside. Continue making 1 more patty for a small batch, 3 more for a medium batch, or 5 more for a larger one, coating them with vegetable oil spray on both sides.
4. Set the patties in one layer in the basket and air-fry undisturbed for 10 minutes, or until lightly browned and cooked through.
5. Use a nonstick-safe spatula to transfer the crab cakes to a serving platter or plates. Wait a couple of minutes before serving.

Variations & Ingredients Tips:

- Add some Old Bay seasoning or Cajun spice to the mix.
- Form into mini crab cakes and serve as an appetizer.
- Serve with a lemon-caper aioli or spicy remoulade sauce.

Per Serving: Calories: 200; Total Fat: 12g; Saturated Fat: 2.5g; Cholesterol: 85mg; Sodium: 720mg; Total Carbs: 10g; Dietary Fiber: 1g; Total Sugars: 2g; Protein: 15g

Fried Scallops

Servings: 3 | Prep Time: 10 Minutes | Cooking Time: 6 Minutes

Ingredients:

- 1/2 cup All-purpose flour or tapioca flour
- 1 Large egg, well beaten
- 2 cups Corn flake crumbs
- Up to 2 teaspoons Cayenne
- 1 teaspoon Celery seeds
- 1 teaspoon Table salt
- 450g Sea scallops
- Vegetable oil spray

Directions:

1. Preheat air fryer to 200°C/400°F.
2. Set up 3 dishes: one with flour, one with beaten egg, one with corn flake crumbs+cayenne+celery seeds+salt.
3. Dip scallops in flour, then egg, then corn flake mix to fully coat.
4. Generously spray scallops with oil on all sides.
5. Arrange scallops in air fryer basket with space between. Do not overcrowd.
6. Air fry for 6 minutes until lightly browned and firm.
7. Transfer to a wire rack and let cool 1-2 minutes before serving.

Variations & Ingredients Tips:

- Use panko breadcrumbs instead of corn flakes.
- Add Old Bay seasoning or lemon zest to the coating mix.
- Serve with lemon wedges or remoulade sauce.

Per Serving: Calories: 318; Total Fat: 2g; Saturated Fat: 1g; Cholesterol: 152mg; Sodium: 767mg; Total Carbs: 44g; Dietary Fiber: 1g; Total Sugars: 3g; Protein: 28g

Flounder Fillets

Servings: 4 | Prep Time: 10 Minutes | Cooking Time: 8 Minutes

Ingredients:

- 1 egg white
- 1 tablespoon water
- 1 cup panko breadcrumbs
- 2 tablespoons extra-light virgin olive oil
- 4 (115g) flounder fillets
- Salt and pepper
- Oil for misting or cooking spray

Directions:

1. Preheat air fryer to 195°C/390°F.
2. Beat together egg white and water in shallow dish.
3. In another shallow dish, mix panko crumbs and oil until well combined and crumbly (best done by hand).
4. Season flounder fillets with salt and pepper to taste. Dip each fillet into egg mixture and then roll in panko crumbs, pressing in crumbs so that fish is nicely coated.

5. Spray air fryer basket with nonstick cooking spray and add fillets. Cook at 195°C/390°F for 3 minutes.
6. Spray fish fillets but do not turn. Cook 5 minutes longer or until golden brown and crispy. Using a spatula, carefully remove fish from basket and serve.

Variations & Ingredients Tips:

- Use cod, sole or tilapia instead of flounder.
- Add some grated Parmesan or lemon zest to the panko breading.
- Serve with tartar sauce, lemon wedges and steamed vegetables.

Per Serving: Calories: 230; Total Fat: 8g; Saturated Fat: 1.5g; Cholesterol: 75mg; Sodium: 300mg; Total Carbs: 13g; Dietary Fiber: 1g; Total Sugars: 1g; Protein: 25g

Chinese Firecracker Shrimp

Servings: 4 | Prep Time: 10 Minutes | Cooking Time: 20 Minutes

Ingredients:

- 450g peeled shrimp, deveined
- 2 green onions, chopped
- 2 tbsp sesame seeds
- Salt and pepper to taste
- 1 egg
- ½ cup all-purpose flour
- ¾ cup panko bread crumbs
- 1/3 cup sour cream
- 2 tbsp Sriracha sauce
- ¼ cup sweet chili sauce

Directions:

1. Preheat air fryer to 200°C/400°F.
2. Set up 3 bowls: one with flour, one with beaten egg, one with panko crumbs.
3. Season shrimp with salt and pepper.
4. Dredge shrimp in flour, then egg, then breadcrumbs to coat.
5. Place shrimp in greased air fryer basket and cook for 8 minutes, flipping once, until crispy.
6. Combine sour cream, Sriracha and sweet chili sauce in a bowl.
7. Top cooked shrimp with sesame seeds and green onions.
8. Serve shrimp with chili dipping sauce.

Variations & Ingredients Tips:

- Use egg roll wrappers cut into strips instead of breadcrumbs for the coating.
- Add garlic, ginger or lime zest to the shrimp before breading.
- Toss cooked shrimp in the sauce instead of serving it on the side.

Per Serving: Calories: 261; Total Fat: 7g; Saturated Fat: 2g; Cholesterol: 194mg; Sodium: 678mg; Total Carbs: 31g; Dietary Fiber: 1g; Total Sugars: 4g; Protein: 19g

Fish Goujons With Tartar Sauce

Servings: 4 | Prep Time: 10 Minutes | Cooking Time: 20 Minutes

Ingredients:

- 1/4 cup flour
- Salt and pepper to taste
- 1/4 tsp smoked paprika
- 1/4 tsp dried oregano
- 1 tsp dried thyme
- 1 egg
- 4 haddock fillets
- 1 lemon, thinly sliced
- 1/2 cup tartar sauce

Directions:

1. Preheat air fryer to 200°C/400°F.
2. Combine flour, salt, pepper, paprika, thyme, and oregano in a wide bowl. Whisk egg and 1 teaspoon water in another wide bowl.
3. Slice each fillet into 4 strips. Dip the strips in the egg mixture. Then roll them in the flour mixture and coat completely.
4. Arrange the fish strips on the greased frying basket. Air Fry for 4 minutes. Flip the fish and Air Fry for another 4 to 5 minutes until crisp.
5. Serve warm with lemon slices and tartar sauce on the side and enjoy.

Variations & Ingredients Tips:

- Use cod, pollack or tilapia instead of haddock.
- Season the flour with Old Bay, lemon pepper or Cajun spice.
- Serve with malt vinegar, coleslaw or mushy peas.

Per Serving: Calories: 330; Total Fat: 17g; Saturated Fat: 2.5g; Cholesterol: 140mg; Sodium: 570mg; Total Carbs: 14g; Dietary Fiber: 1g; Total Sugars: 1g; Protein: 30g

Vegetarian Recipes

Tropical Salsa

Servings: 4 | Prep Time: 10 Minutes | Cooking Time: 15 Minutes

Ingredients:

- 1 cup pineapple cubes
- ½ apple, cubed
- Salt to taste
- ¼ tsp olive oil
- 2 tomatoes, diced
- 1 avocado, diced
- 3-4 strawberries, diced
- ¼ cup diced red onion
- 1 tbsp chopped cilantro
- 1 tbsp chopped parsley
- 2 cloves garlic, minced
- ½ tsp granulated sugar
- ½ lime, juiced

Directions:

1. Preheat air fryer at 200°C/400°F.
2. Combine pineapple cubes, apples, olive oil, and salt in a bowl. Place pineapple in the greased air fryer basket, and Air Fry for 8 minutes, shaking once. Transfer it to a bowl.
3. Toss in tomatoes, avocado, strawberries, onion, cilantro, parsley, garlic, sugar, lime juice, and salt. Let chill in the fridge before using.

Variations & Ingredients Tips:

- Add diced mango, papaya, or kiwi for more tropical flavor.
- Substitute lime juice with orange or lemon juice.
- Serve with tortilla chips or as a topping for tacos, burritos, or salads.

Per Serving: Calories: 120; Total Fat: 6g; Saturated Fat: 1g; Sodium: 150mg; Total Carbohydrates: 18g; Dietary Fiber: 5g; Total Sugars: 11g; Protein: 2g

Rainbow Quinoa Patties

Servings: 4 | Prep Time: 10 Minutes | Cooking Time: 20 Minutes

Ingredients:

- 1 cup canned tri-bean blend, drained and rinsed
- 2 tbsp olive oil
- ½ tsp ground cumin
- ½ tsp garlic salt
- 1 tbsp paprika
- 1/3 cup uncooked quinoa
- 2 tbsp chopped onion
- ¼ cup shredded carrot
- 2 tbsp chopped cilantro
- 1 tsp chili powder
- ½ tsp salt
- 2 tbsp mascarpone cheese

Directions:

1. Place 1/3 cup of water, 1 tbsp of olive oil, cumin, and salt in a saucepan over medium heat and bring it to a boil. Remove from the heat and stir in quinoa. Let rest covered for 5 minutes.
2. Preheat air fryer at 180°C/350°F.
3. Using the back of a fork, mash beans until smooth. Toss in cooked quinoa and the remaining ingredients.
4. Form mixture into 4 patties. Place patties in the greased air fryer basket and Air Fry for 6 minutes, turning once, and brush with the remaining olive oil.
5. Serve immediately.

Variations & Ingredients Tips:

- Use any combination of canned beans like black beans, kidney beans, or chickpeas.
- Add grated zucchini or sweet potato for extra moisture and nutrients.
- Serve with yogurt dip or guacamole.

Per Serving: Calories: 240; Total Fat: 12g; Saturated Fat: 3g; Sodium: 660mg; Total Carbohydrates: 26g; Dietary Fiber: 6g; Total Sugars: 2g; Protein: 8g

Sweet Corn Bread

Servings: 6 | Prep Time: 10 Minutes | Cooking Time: 35 Minutes

Ingredients:

- 2 eggs, beaten
- ½ cup cornmeal
- ½ cup pastry flour
- 1/3 cup sugar
- 1 tsp lemon zest
- ½ tbsp baking powder
- ¼ tsp salt
- ¼ tsp baking soda
- ½ tbsp lemon juice
- ½ cup milk
- ¼ cup sunflower oil

Directions:

1. Preheat air fryer to 180°C/350°F.
2. Add the cornmeal, flour, sugar, lemon zest, baking powder, salt, and baking soda in a bowl. Stir with a whisk until combined.
3. Add the eggs, lemon juice, milk, and oil to another bowl and stir well. Add the wet mixture to the dry mixture and stir gently until combined.
4. Spray a baking pan with oil. Pour the batter in and Bake in the fryer for 25 minutes or until golden and a knife inserted in the center comes out clean.
5. Cut into wedges and serve.

Variations & Ingredients Tips:

- Add grated cheddar cheese, diced jalapeños, or corn kernels to the batter.
- Substitute lemon with orange or lime for a different citrus flavor.
- Serve with honey butter or maple syrup.

Per Serving: Calories: 240; Total Fat: 11g; Saturated Fat: 1.5g; Sodium: 290mg; Total Carbohydrates: 32g; Dietary Fiber: 1g; Total Sugars: 14g; Protein: 5g

Pineapple & Veggie Souvlaki

Servings: 4 | Prep Time: 20 Minutes | Cooking Time: 35 Minutes

Ingredients:

- 1 can pineapple rings in pineapple juice
- 1 red bell pepper, stemmed and seeded
- 1/3 cup butter
- 2 tbsp apple cider vinegar
- 2 tbsp hot sauce
- 1 tbsp allspice
- 1 tsp ground nutmeg
- 454 grams feta cheese
- 1 red onion, peeled
- 8 mushrooms, quartered

Directions:

1. Preheat air fryer to 200°C/400°F.
2. Whisk the butter, pineapple juice, apple vinegar, hot sauce, allspice, and nutmeg until smooth. Set aside.
3. Slice feta cheese into 16 cubes, then the bell pepper into 16 chunks, and finally red onion into 8 wedges, separating each wedge into 2 pieces.
4. Cut pineapple ring into quarters. Place veggie cubes and feta into the butter bowl and toss to coat.
5. Thread the veggies, tofu, and pineapple onto 8 skewers, alternating 16 pieces on each skewer.
6. Grill for 15 minutes until golden brown and cooked. Serve warm.

Variations & Ingredients Tips:

- Use halloumi cheese instead of feta for a firmer texture.
- Add zucchini, cherry tomatoes, or eggplant chunks to the skewers.
- Brush skewers with any leftover marinade during cooking for extra flavor.

Per Serving: Calories: 420; Total Fat: 33g; Saturated Fat: 21g; Sodium: 1120mg; Total Carbohydrates: 16g; Dietary Fiber: 2g; Total Sugars: 12g; Protein: 17g

Cauliflower Steaks Gratin

Servings: 2 | Prep Time: 10 Minutes | Cooking Time: 13 Minutes

Ingredients:

- 1 head cauliflower
- 1 tablespoon olive oil
- salt and freshly ground black pepper
- ½ teaspoon chopped fresh thyme leaves
- 3 tablespoons grated Parmigiano-Reggiano cheese
- 2 tablespoons panko breadcrumbs

Directions:

1. Preheat the air-fryer to 190°C/370°F.
2. Cut two steaks out of the center of the cauliflower. To do this, cut the cauliflower in half and then cut one slice about 5-cm thick off each half. The rest of the cauliflower will fall apart into florets, which you can roast on their own or save for another meal.
3. Brush both sides of the cauliflower steaks with olive oil and season with salt, freshly ground black pepper and fresh thyme. Place the cauliflower steaks into the air fryer basket and air-fry for 6 minutes. Turn the steaks over and air-fry for another 4 minutes. Combine the Parmesan cheese and panko breadcrumbs and sprinkle the mixture over the tops of both steaks and air-fry for another 3 minutes until the cheese has melted and the breadcrumbs have browned. Serve this with some sautéed bitter greens and air-fried blistered tomatoes.

Variations & Ingredients Tips:

- Use different herbs like rosemary, oregano, or basil for a variety of flavors.
- Add minced garlic or red pepper flakes to the oil mixture for extra kick.
- Substitute Parmesan with Gruyère, Pecorino, or Asiago cheese for a different taste.

Per Serving (1 cauliflower steak): Calories: 190; Cholesterol: 10mg; Total Fat: 12g; Saturated Fat: 4g; Sodium: 420mg; Total Carbohydrates: 13g; Dietary Fiber: 5g; Total Sugars: 5g; Protein: 9g

Farfalle With White Sauce

Servings: 4 | Prep Time: 10 Minutes | Cooking Time: 30 Minutes

Ingredients:

- 4 cups cauliflower florets
- 1 medium onion, chopped
- 225g farfalle pasta
- 2 tbsp chives, minced
- 1/2 cup cashew pieces
- 1 tbsp nutritional yeast
- 2 large garlic cloves, peeled
- 2 tbsp fresh lemon juice
- Salt and pepper to taste

Directions:

1. Preheat air fryer to 200°C/390°F. Put the cauliflower in the fryer, spray with oil, and Bake for 8 minutes. Remove the basket, stir, and add the onion. Roast for 10 minutes or until the cauliflower is golden and the onions soft.
2. Cook the farfalle pasta according to the package directions. Set aside.
3. Put the roasted cauliflower and onions along with the cashews, 1 1/2 cups of water, yeast, garlic, lemon, salt, and pepper in a blender. Blend until creamy.
4. Pour a large portion of the sauce on top of the warm pasta and add the minced scallions. Serve.

Variations & Ingredients Tips:

- Add roasted garlic for extra flavor depth.
- Substitute cashews with toasted almonds or pine nuts.
- Toss in sautéed spinach or kale for added nutrients.

Per Serving: Calories: 390; Total Fat: 13g; Saturated Fat: 2g; Sodium: 130mg; Total Carbs: 58g; Dietary Fiber: 6g; Total Sugars: 6g; Protein: 14g

Colorful Vegetable Medley

Servings: 4 | Prep Time: 10 Minutes | Cooking Time: 20 Minutes

Ingredients:

- 455g green beans, chopped
- 2 carrots, cubed
- Salt and pepper to taste
- 1 zucchini, cut into chunks
- 1 red bell pepper, sliced

Directions:

1. Preheat air fryer to 200°C/390°F. Combine green beans, carrots, salt and pepper in a large bowl. Spray with cooking oil and transfer to the frying basket. Roast for 6 minutes.
2. Combine zucchini and red pepper in a bowl. Season to taste and spray with cooking oil; set aside. When the cooking time is up, add the zucchini and red pepper to the basket. Cook for another 6 minutes.
3. Serve and enjoy.

Variations & Ingredients Tips:

- Add diced potatoes or sweet potatoes for extra heartiness.
- Substitute green beans with asparagus or broccolini.
- Toss with balsamic vinegar or lemon juice before serving for extra flavor.

Per Serving: Calories 80, Total Fat 0.5g, Saturated Fat 0g, Cholesterol 0mg, Sodium 70mg, Total Carbs 16g, Dietary Fiber 6g, Total Sugars 8g, Protein 4g

Italian-style Fried Cauliflower

Servings: 4 | Prep Time: 25 Minutes | Cooking Time: 35 Minutes

Ingredients:

- 2 eggs
- 1/3 cup all-purpose flour
- ½ tsp Italian seasoning
- ½ cup bread crumbs
- 1 tsp garlic powder
- 3 tsp grated Parmesan cheese
- Salt and pepper to taste
- 1 head cauliflower, cut into florets
- ½ tsp ground coriander

Directions:

1. Preheat air fryer to 190°C/370°F.
2. Set out 3 small bowls. In the first, mix the flour with Italian seasoning. In the second, beat the eggs. In the third bowl, combine the crumbs, garlic, Parmesan, ground coriander, salt, and pepper.
3. Dip the cauliflower in the flour, then dredge in egg, and finally in the bread crumb mixture.
4. Place a batch of cauliflower in the greased air fryer basket and spray with cooking oil.
5. Bake for 10-12 minutes, shaking once until golden.
6. Serve warm and enjoy!

Variations & Ingredients Tips:

- Use panko breadcrumbs for an extra crispy texture.
- Add red pepper flakes or cayenne to the breading for a spicy kick.
- Serve with marinara sauce or ranch dressing for dipping.

Per Serving: Calories: 170; Total Fat: 5g; Saturated Fat: 1.5g; Sodium: 410mg; Total Carbohydrates: 24g; Dietary Fiber: 5g; Total Sugars: 4g; Protein: 9g

Stuffed Portobellos

Servings: 4 | Prep Time: 20 Minutes | Cooking Time: 45 Minutes

Ingredients:

- 1 cup cherry tomatoes
- 2 ¼ tsp olive oil
- 3 tbsp grated mozzarella
- 1 cup chopped baby spinach
- 1 garlic clove, minced
- ¼ tsp dried oregano
- ¼ tsp dried thyme
- Salt and pepper to taste
- ¼ cup bread crumbs
- 4 portobello mushrooms, stemmed and gills removed
- 1 tbsp chopped parsley

Directions:

1. Preheat air fryer to 180°C/360°F.
2. Combine tomatoes, ¼ teaspoon olive oil, and salt in a small bowl. Arrange in a single layer in the parchment-lined air fryer basket and Air Fry for 10 minutes. Stir and flatten the tomatoes with the back of a spoon, then Air Fry for another 6-8 minutes.
3. Transfer the tomatoes to a medium bowl and combine with spinach, garlic, oregano, thyme, pepper, bread crumbs, and the rest of the olive oil.
4. Place the mushrooms on a work surface with the gills facing up. Spoon tomato mixture and mozzarella cheese equally into the mushroom caps and transfer the mushrooms to the air fryer basket.
5. Air Fry for 8-10 minutes until the mushrooms have softened and the tops are golden.
6. Garnish with chopped parsley and serve.

Variations & Ingredients Tips:

- Substitute portobello mushrooms with large button mushrooms or zucchini boats.
- Add cooked quinoa, rice, or ground meat to the filling for a heartier dish.
- Top with a drizzle of balsamic glaze or pesto sauce before serving.

Per Serving: Calories: 130; Total Fat: 7g; Saturated Fat: 2g; Sodium: 200mg; Total Carbohydrates: 12g; Dietary Fiber: 3g; Total Sugars: 4g; Protein: 7g

Egg Rolls

Servings: 4 | Prep Time: 20 Minutes | Cooking Time: 8 Minutes

Ingredients:

- 1 clove garlic, minced
- 1 teaspoon sesame oil
- 1 teaspoon olive oil

- ½ cup chopped celery
- ½ cup grated carrots
- 2 green onions, chopped
- 55 grams mushrooms, chopped
- 2 cups shredded Napa cabbage
- 1 teaspoon low-sodium soy sauce
- 1 teaspoon cornstarch
- salt
- 1 egg
- 1 tablespoon water
- 4 egg roll wraps
- olive oil for misting or cooking spray

Directions:

1. In a large skillet, sauté garlic in sesame and olive oils over medium heat for 1 minute.
2. Add celery, carrots, onions, and mushrooms to skillet. Cook 1 minute, stirring.
3. Stir in cabbage, cover, and cook for 1 minute or just until cabbage slightly wilts.
4. In a small bowl, mix soy sauce and cornstarch. Stir into vegetables to thicken. Remove from heat. Salt to taste if needed.
5. Beat together egg and water in a small bowl.
6. Divide filling into 4 portions and roll up in egg roll wraps. Brush all over with egg wash to seal.
7. Mist egg rolls very lightly with olive oil or cooking spray and place in air fryer basket.
8. Cook at 200°C/390°F for 4 minutes. Turn over and cook 4 more minutes, until golden brown and crispy.

Variations & Ingredients Tips:

- Use ground pork, chicken, or tofu for a protein-packed filling.
- Add bean sprouts, bamboo shoots, or water chestnuts for extra crunch.
- Serve with sweet and sour sauce, hoisin sauce, or hot mustard for dipping.

Per Serving (1 egg roll): Calories: 140; Cholesterol: 50mg; Total Fat: 5g; Saturated Fat: 1g; Sodium: 300mg; Total Carbohydrates: 18g; Dietary Fiber: 2g; Total Sugars: 2g; Protein: 5g

Spicy Bean Patties

Servings: 4 | Prep Time: 10 Minutes | Cooking Time: 20 Minutes

Ingredients:

- 1 cup canned black beans
- 1 bread slice, torn
- 2 tbsp spicy brown mustard
- 1 tbsp chili powder
- 1 egg white
- 2 tbsp grated carrots
- ¼ diced green bell pepper
- 1-2 jalapeño peppers, diced
- ¼ tsp ground cumin
- ¼ tsp smoked paprika
- 2 tbsp cream cheese
- 1 tbsp olive oil

Directions:

1. Preheat air fryer at 180°C/350°F.
2. Using a fork, mash beans until smooth. Stir in the remaining ingredients, except olive oil.
3. Form mixture into 4 patties.
4. Place bean patties in the greased air fryer basket and Air Fry for 6 minutes, turning once, and brush with olive oil.
5. Serve immediately.

Variations & Ingredients Tips:

- Use any type of canned beans like pinto, kidney, or white beans.
- Add minced garlic or onion for extra flavor.
- Serve on a bun with lettuce, tomato, and avocado for a veggie burger.

Per Serving: Calories: 150; Total Fat: 6g; Saturated Fat: 2g; Sodium: 360mg; Total Carbohydrates: 18g; Dietary Fiber: 5g; Total Sugars: 2g; Protein: 7g

Easy Cheese & Spinach Lasagna

Servings: 6 | Prep Time: 20 Minutes | Cooking Time: 50 Minutes

Ingredients:

- 1 zucchini, cut into strips
- 1 tbsp butter
- 4 garlic cloves, minced
- ½ yellow onion, diced
- 1 tsp dried oregano
- ¼ tsp red pepper flakes
- 1 can diced tomatoes
- 115 grams ricotta
- 3 tbsp grated mozzarella
- ½ cup grated cheddar
- 3 tsp grated Parmesan cheese

- ⅛ cup chopped basil
- 2 tbsp chopped parsley
- Salt and pepper to taste
- ¼ tsp ground nutmeg

Directions:

1. Preheat air fryer to 190°C/375°F. Melt butter in a medium skillet over medium heat. Stir in half of the garlic and onion and cook for 2 minutes. Stir in oregano and red pepper flakes and cook for 1 minute. Reduce the heat to medium-low and pour in crushed tomatoes and their juices. Cover the skillet and simmer for 5 minutes.
2. Mix ricotta, mozzarella, cheddar cheese, rest of the garlic, basil, black pepper, and nutmeg in a large bowl. Arrange a layer of zucchini strips in the baking dish. Scoop 1/3 of the cheese mixture and spread evenly over the zucchini. Spread 1/3 of the tomato sauce over the cheese. Repeat the steps two more times, then top the lasagna with Parmesan cheese. Bake in the frying basket for 25 minutes until the mixture is bubbling and the mozzarella is melted. Allow sitting for 10 minutes before cutting. Serve warm sprinkled with parsley and enjoy!

Variations & Ingredients Tips:

- Add sliced mushrooms, bell peppers, or eggplant to the veggie layers for extra nutrition.
- Substitute ricotta with cottage cheese or tofu for a different texture.
- Use a jar of your favorite pasta sauce instead of making the tomato sauce from scratch.

Per Serving: Calories: 250; Cholesterol: 40mg; Total Fat: 16g; Saturated Fat: 9g; Sodium: 520mg; Total Carbohydrates: 15g; Dietary Fiber: 3g; Total Sugars: 7g; Protein: 14g

Kale & Lentils With Crispy Onions

Servings: 4 | Prep Time: 20 Minutes | Cooking Time: 40 Minutes

Ingredients:

- 2 cups cooked red lentils
- 1 onion, cut into rings
- ½ cup kale, steamed
- 3 garlic cloves, minced
- ½ lemon, juiced and zested
- 2 tsp cornstarch
- 1 tsp dried oregano
- Salt and pepper to taste

Directions:

1. Preheat air fryer to 200°C/390°F.
2. Put the onion rings in the greased air fryer basket; do not overlap. Spray with oil and season with salt. Air Fry for 14-16 minutes, stirring twice until crispy and crunchy.
3. Place the kale and lentils into a pan over medium heat and stir until heated through.
4. Remove and add the garlic, lemon juice, cornstarch, salt, zest, oregano and black pepper. Stir well and pour in bowls.
5. Top with the crisp onion rings and serve.

Variations & Ingredients Tips:

- Use spinach or Swiss chard instead of kale.
- Add chopped sun-dried tomatoes or roasted red peppers for sweetness.
- Top with grated Parmesan cheese or nutritional yeast.

Per Serving: Calories: 240; Total Fat: 2g; Saturated Fat: 0g; Sodium: 160mg; Total Carbohydrates: 40g; Dietary Fiber: 17g; Total Sugars: 4g; Protein: 18g

Vietnamese Gingered Tofu

Servings: 4 | Prep Time: 10 Minutes | Cooking Time: 25 Minutes

Ingredients:

- 1 package extra-firm tofu, cubed
- 4 tsp shoyu (soy sauce)
- 1 tsp onion powder
- 1/2 tsp garlic powder
- 1/2 tsp ginger powder
- 1/2 tsp turmeric powder
- Black pepper to taste
- 2 tbsp nutritional yeast
- 1 tsp dried rosemary
- 1 tsp dried dill
- 2 tsp cornstarch
- 2 tsp sunflower oil

Directions:

1. Sprinkle the tofu with shoyu and toss to coat.
2. Add the onion, garlic, ginger, turmeric, and pepper. Gently toss to coat.

3. Add the yeast, rosemary, dill, and cornstarch. Toss to coat.
4. Dribble with the oil and toss again.
5. Preheat air fryer to 200°C/390°F. Spray the basket with oil.
6. Put the tofu in the basket and Bake for 7 minutes.
7. Remove, shake gently, and cook for another 7 minutes or until crispy and golden.
8. Serve warm.

Variations & Ingredients Tips:

- Use tamari or coconut aminos instead of soy sauce.
- Add chili garlic sauce or sriracha for a spicy kick.
- Toss with chopped scallions before serving.

Per Serving: Calories: 132; Total Fat: 7g; Saturated Fat: 1g; Sodium: 514mg; Total Carbohydrates: 8g; Dietary Fiber: 2g; Total Sugars: 1g; Protein: 13g

Easy Zucchini Lasagna Roll-ups

Servings: 2 | Prep Time: 20 Minutes | Cooking Time: 40 Minutes

Ingredients:

- 2 medium zucchini
- 2 tbsp lemon juice
- 1 ½ cups ricotta cheese
- 1 tbsp allspice
- 2 cups marinara sauce
- 1/3 cup mozzarella cheese

Directions:

1. Preheat air fryer to 200°C/400°F. Cut the ends of each zucchini, then slice into 6-mm thick pieces and drizzle with lemon juice. Roast for 5 minutes until slightly tender. Let cool slightly. Combine ricotta cheese and allspice in a bowl; set aside. Spread 2 tbsp of marinara sauce on the bottom of a baking pan. Spoon 1-2 tbsp of the ricotta mixture onto each slice, roll up each slice and place them spiral-side up in the pan. Scatter with the remaining ricotta mixture and drizzle with marinara sauce. Top with mozzarella cheese and Bake at 180°C/360°F for 20 minutes until the cheese is bubbly and golden brown. Serve warm.

Variations & Ingredients Tips:

- Substitute zucchini with eggplant or lasagna noodles for different textures.
- Add minced garlic, basil, or oregano to the ricotta mixture for extra flavor.
- Top with grated Parmesan cheese or breadcrumbs before baking for a crispy crust.

Per Serving: Calories: 470; Cholesterol: 80mg; Total Fat: 25g; Saturated Fat: 15g; Sodium: 1060mg; Total Carbohydrates: 38g; Dietary Fiber: 7g; Total Sugars: 22g; Protein: 29g

Eggplant Parmesan

Servings: 4 | Prep Time: 20 Minutes | Cooking Time: 8 Minutes Per Batch

Ingredients:

- 1 medium eggplant, 15-20 cm long
- salt
- 1 large egg
- 1 tablespoon water
- ⅔ cup panko breadcrumbs
- ⅓ cup grated Parmesan cheese, plus more for serving
- 1 tablespoon Italian seasoning
- ¾ teaspoon oregano
- oil for misting or cooking spray
- 1 680-gram jar marinara sauce
- 225 grams spaghetti, cooked
- pepper

Directions:

1. Preheat air fryer to 200°C/390°F.
2. Leaving peel intact, cut eggplant into 8 round slices about 2-cm thick. Salt to taste.
3. Beat egg and water in a shallow dish.
4. In another shallow dish, combine panko, Parmesan, Italian seasoning, and oregano.
5. Dip eggplant slices in egg wash and then crumbs, pressing lightly to coat.
6. Mist slices with oil or cooking spray.
7. Place 4 eggplant slices in air fryer basket and cook for 8 minutes, until brown and crispy.
8. While eggplant is cooking, heat marinara sauce.
9. Repeat step 7 to cook remaining eggplant slices.
10. To serve, place cooked spaghetti on plates and top with marinara and eggplant slices. At the table, pass extra Parmesan cheese and freshly ground black pepper.

Variations & Ingredients Tips:

- Substitute eggplant with zucchini or portobello mushrooms for a different veggie option.

- Use gluten-free breadcrumbs and pasta for a gluten-free version.
- Serve with a side salad or garlic bread for a complete meal.

Per Serving: Calories: 420; Cholesterol: 55mg; Total Fat: 11g; Saturated Fat: 3g; Sodium: 1180mg; Total Carbohydrates: 68g; Dietary Fiber: 9g; Total Sugars: 16g; Protein: 16g

Crispy Apple Fries With Caramel Sauce

Servings: 4 | Prep Time: 10 Minutes | Cooking Time: 15 Minutes

Ingredients:

- 4 medium apples, cored
- ¼ tsp cinnamon
- ¼ tsp nutmeg
- 1 cup caramel sauce

Directions:

1. Preheat air fryer to 175°C/350°F. Slice the apples to a 8-mm thickness for a crunchy chip. Place in a large bowl and sprinkle with cinnamon and nutmeg. Place the slices in the air fryer basket. Bake for 6 minutes. Shake the basket, then cook for another 4 minutes or until crunchy. Serve drizzled with caramel sauce and enjoy!

Variations & Ingredients Tips:

- Use different apple varieties like Granny Smith, Honeycrisp, or Fuji for varied flavors.
- Substitute caramel sauce with melted chocolate or peanut butter for a different dip.
- Sprinkle with chopped nuts or granola for extra crunch.

Per Serving: Calories: 310; Cholesterol: 15mg; Total Fat: 6g; Saturated Fat: 3.5g; Sodium: 260mg; Total Carbohydrates: 64g; Dietary Fiber: 5g; Total Sugars: 51g; Protein: 1g

Vegetable Couscous

Servings: 4 | Prep Time: 10 Minutes | Cooking Time: 10 Minutes

Ingredients:

- 113g white mushrooms, sliced
- 1/2 medium green bell pepper, julienned
- 1 cup cubed zucchini
- 1/4 small onion, slivered
- 1 stalk celery, thinly sliced
- 1/4 teaspoon ground coriander
- 1/4 teaspoon ground cumin
- Salt and pepper
- 1 tablespoon olive oil
- 3/4 cup uncooked couscous
- 1 cup vegetable broth or water
- 1/2 teaspoon salt (omit if using salted broth)

Directions:

1. Combine all vegetables in a large bowl. Sprinkle with coriander, cumin, and salt and pepper to taste. Stir well, add olive oil, and stir again to coat vegetables evenly.
2. Place vegetables in the air fryer basket and cook at 200°C/390°F for 5 minutes. Stir and cook for 5 more minutes, until tender.
3. While vegetables are cooking, prepare the couscous: Place broth or water and salt in a large saucepan. Heat to boiling, stir in couscous, cover, and remove from heat.
4. Let couscous sit for 5 minutes, stir in cooked vegetables, and serve hot.

Variations & Ingredients Tips:

- Add chickpeas or lentils for extra protein.
- Use different fresh or dried herbs like parsley, thyme or oregano.
- Toss in some feta or goat cheese for a creamy touch.

Per Serving: Calories: 189; Total Fat: 6g; Saturated Fat: 1g; Sodium: 395mg; Total Carbohydrates: 29g; Dietary Fiber: 4g; Total Sugars: 3g; Protein: 6g

Tortilla Pizza Margherita

Servings: 1 | Prep Time: 5 Minutes | Cooking Time: 15 Minutes

Ingredients:

- 1 flour tortilla
- ¼ cup tomato sauce
- 1/3 cup grated mozzarella
- 3 basil leaves

Directions:

1. Preheat air fryer to 180°C/350°F.
2. Put the tortilla in the greased basket and pour the sauce in the center. Spread across the whole tortilla.
3. Sprinkle with cheese and Bake for 8-10 minutes or until crisp.
4. Remove carefully and top with basil leaves. Serve hot.

Variations & Ingredients Tips:

- Add sliced cherry tomatoes, olives, or mushrooms as additional toppings.
- Use pesto sauce instead of tomato sauce for a green pizza.
- Sprinkle with red pepper flakes or dried oregano for extra seasoning.

Per Serving: Calories: 290; Total Fat: 12g; Saturated Fat: 5g; Sodium: 780mg; Total Carbohydrates: 31g; Dietary Fiber: 2g; Total Sugars: 4g; Protein: 14g

Smoky Sweet Potato Fries

Servings: 4 | Prep Time: 10 Minutes | Cooking Time: 25 Minutes

Ingredients:

- 2 large sweet potatoes, peeled and sliced
- 1 tbsp olive oil
- Salt and pepper to taste
- ¼ tsp garlic powder
- ¼ tsp smoked paprika
- 1 tbsp pumpkin pie spice
- 1 tbsp chopped parsley

Directions:

1. Preheat air fryer to 190°C/375°F.
2. Toss sweet potato slices, olive oil, salt, pepper, garlic powder, pumpkin pie spice and paprika in a large bowl.
3. Arrange the potatoes in a single layer in the air fryer basket.
4. Air Fry for 5 minutes, then shake the basket.
5. Air Fry for another 5 minutes and shake the basket again.
6. Air Fry for 2-5 minutes until crispy.
7. Serve sprinkled with parsley and enjoy.

Variations & Ingredients Tips:

- Cut the sweet potatoes into wedges or rounds for different shapes.
- Substitute pumpkin pie spice with cinnamon or nutmeg for a simpler flavor.
- Serve with a dipping sauce like sriracha mayo or garlic aioli.

Per Serving: Calories: 130; Total Fat: 4g; Saturated Fat: 0.5g; Sodium: 135mg; Total Carbohydrates: 23g; Dietary Fiber: 4g; Total Sugars: 6g; Protein: 2g

Vegetable Side Dishes Recipes

Goat Cheese Stuffed Portobellos

Servings: 4 | Prep Time: 15 Minutes | Cooking Time: 35 Minutes

Ingredients:

- 1 cup baby spinach
- 3/4 cup crumbled goat cheese
- 2 tsp grated Parmesan cheese
- 4 portobello caps, cleaned
- Salt and pepper to taste
- 2 tomatoes, chopped
- 1 leek, chopped
- 1 garlic clove, minced
- 1/4 cup chopped parsley
- 2 tbsp panko bread crumbs
- 1 tbsp chopped oregano
- 1 tbsp olive oil
- Balsamic glaze for drizzling

Directions:

1. Brush the mushrooms with olive oil and sprinkle with salt.
2. Mix the remaining ingredients, excluding the balsamic glaze, in a bowl.
3. Fill each mushroom cap with the mixture.
4. Preheat air fryer to 190°C/370°F.
5. Place the mushroom caps in the greased frying basket and bake for 10-12 minutes or until the top is golden and the mushrooms are tender.
6. Carefully transfer them to a serving dish. Drizzle with balsamic glaze and serve warm.

Variations & Ingredients Tips:

- Add crumbled bacon or sausage to the stuffing for extra flavor.
- Substitute feta or ricotta cheese for the goat cheese.
- Use breadcrumbs instead of panko for a different texture.

Per Serving: Calories: 190; Total Fat: 12g; Saturated Fat: 6g; Cholesterol: 20mg; Sodium: 240mg; Total Carbohydrates: 12g; Dietary Fiber: 3g; Total Sugars: 5g; Protein: 10g

Blistered Green Beans

Servings: 3 | Prep Time: 5 Minutes | Cooking Time: 10 Minutes

Ingredients:

- 340g Green beans, trimmed on both ends
- 1½ tablespoons Olive oil
- 3 tablespoons Pine nuts
- 1½ tablespoons Balsamic vinegar
- 1½ teaspoons Minced garlic
- ¾ teaspoon Table salt
- ¾ teaspoon Ground black pepper

Directions:

1. Preheat the air fryer to 200°C/400°F.
2. Toss the green beans and oil in a large bowl until all the green beans are glistening.
3. When the machine is at temperature, pile the green beans into the basket. Air-fry for 10 minutes, tossing often to rearrange the green beans in the basket, or until blistered and tender.
4. Dump the contents of the basket into a serving bowl. Add the pine nuts, vinegar, garlic, salt, and pepper. Toss well to coat and combine. Serve warm or at room temperature.

Variations & Ingredients Tips:

- Add crushed red pepper flakes for a kick of heat.
- Substitute walnuts or sliced almonds for the pine nuts.
- Toss with grated parmesan before serving.

Per Serving: Calories: 150; Total Fat: 11g; Saturated Fat: 1g; Cholesterol: 0mg; Sodium: 460mg; Total Carbs: 10g; Fiber: 4g; Sugars: 4g; Protein: 4g

Hasselback Garlic-and-butter Potatoes

Servings: 3 | Prep Time: 10 Minutes | Cooking Time: 48 Minutes

Ingredients:

- 3 (227g) russet potatoes
- 6 brown button or baby bella mushrooms, very thinly sliced
- Olive oil spray
- 3 tablespoons butter, melted and cooled
- 1 tablespoon minced garlic
- 3/4 teaspoon table salt
- 3 tablespoons (about 14g) finely grated Parmesan cheese

Directions:

1. Preheat the air fryer to 180°C/350°F.
2. Cut slits down the length of each potato, about three-quarters down into the potato and spaced about 6mm apart. Wedge a thin mushroom slice in each slit. Generously coat the potatoes on all sides with olive oil spray.
3. When the machine is at temperature, set the potatoes mushroom side up in the basket with as much air space between them as possible. Air-fry undisturbed for 45 minutes, or tender when pricked with a fork.
4. Increase the machine's temperature to 200°C/400°F. Use kitchen tongs, and perhaps a flatware fork for balance, to gently transfer the potatoes to a cutting board. Brush each evenly with butter, then sprinkle the minced garlic and salt over them. Sprinkle the cheese evenly over the potatoes.
5. Use those same tongs to gently transfer the potatoes cheese side up to the basket in one layer with some space for air flow between them. Air-fry undisturbed for 3 minutes, or until the cheese has melted and begun to brown.
6. Use those same tongs to gently transfer the potatoes

back to the wire rack. Cool for 5 minutes before serving.

Variations & Ingredients Tips:

- Use sweet potatoes instead of russets.
- Mix herbs like rosemary or thyme into the melted butter.
- Top with crispy bacon bits after baking.

Per Serving: Calories: 280; Total Fat: 16g; Saturated Fat: 8g; Cholesterol: 35mg; Sodium: 650mg; Total Carbohydrates: 32g; Dietary Fiber: 3g; Total Sugars: 1g; Protein: 6g

Moroccan-spiced Carrots

Servings: 4 | Prep Time: 5 Minutes | Cooking Time: 30 Minutes

Ingredients:

- 567g baby carrots
- 2 tablespoons butter, melted and cooled
- 1 teaspoon smoked paprika
- 1 teaspoon ground cumin
- 3/4 teaspoon ground coriander
- 3/4 teaspoon ground ginger
- 1/4 teaspoon ground cinnamon
- 1/2 teaspoon table salt
- 1/4 teaspoon ground black pepper

Directions:

1. Preheat the air fryer to 204°C/400°F.
2. Toss the carrots with melted butter, paprika, cumin, coriander, ginger, cinnamon, salt and pepper in a bowl until coated.
3. When machine is at temperature, spread carrots into basket in a single layer.
4. Air fry for 30 minutes, tossing and rearranging every 8 minutes, until crisp-tender and lightly browned in spots.
5. Transfer carrots to a serving bowl and allow to cool for 2 minutes before serving warm or at room temperature.

Variations & Ingredients Tips:

- Add honey or maple syrup for a sweet and spicy flavor.
- Toss with chopped parsley or cilantro after cooking.
- Substitute olive oil for the melted butter.

Per Serving: Calories: 110; Total Fat: 6g; Saturated Fat: 3.5g; Cholesterol: 15mg; Sodium: 370mg; Total Carbohydrates: 14g; Dietary Fiber: 4g; Total Sugars: 8g; Protein: 1g

Garlicky Brussels Sprouts

Servings: 4 | Prep Time: 10 Minutes | Cooking Time: 35 Minutes

Ingredients:

- 454g Brussels sprouts, halved lengthwise
- 1 tbsp olive oil
- 1 tbsp lemon juice
- ½ tsp sea salt
- ⅛ tsp garlic powder
- 4 garlic cloves, sliced
- 2 tbsp parsley, chopped
- ½ tsp red chili flakes

Directions:

1. Preheat air fryer to 190°C/375°F.
2. Combine the olive oil, lemon juice, salt, and garlic powder in a bowl. Add sprouts and toss to coat.
3. Put sprouts in the frying basket. Air Fry 15-20 mins, shaking once until golden and crisp.
4. Sprinkle with garlic slices, parsley, and chili flakes. Toss and cook 2-4 mins more until garlic browns slightly.

Variations & Ingredients Tips:

- Add grated parmesan or panko breadcrumbs for crunch.
- Substitute balsamic vinegar for some of the oil.
- Use pre-shredded brussels sprout pieces for faster cooking.

Per Serving: Calories: 90; Total Fat: 5g; Saturated Fat: 1g; Cholesterol: 0mg; Sodium: 290mg; Total Carbs: 10g; Fiber: 4g; Sugars: 2g; Protein: 4g

Mashed Potato Pancakes

Servings: 6 | Prep Time: 10 Minutes | Cooking Time: 10 Minutes

Ingredients:

- 2 cups leftover mashed potatoes
- 1/2 cup grated cheddar cheese
- 1/4 cup thinly sliced green onions
- 1/2 teaspoon salt

- 1/4 teaspoon black pepper
- 1 cup breadcrumbs

Directions:

1. Preheat the air fryer to 193°C/380°F.
2. In a large bowl, mix together the potatoes, cheese, and onions.
3. Using a 1/4 cup measuring cup, measure out 6 patties. Form the potatoes into 1.25cm thick patties.
4. Season the patties with salt and pepper on both sides.
5. In a small bowl, place the breadcrumbs. Gently press the potato pancakes into the breadcrumbs to coat.
6. Place the potato pancakes into the air fryer basket and spray with cooking spray.
7. Cook for 5 minutes, turn the pancakes over, and cook another 3 to 5 minutes or until golden brown.

Variations & Ingredients Tips:

- Add cooked bacon, chives or garlic to the potato mixture.
- Use panko breadcrumbs for extra crispiness.
- Serve with sour cream, chives or salsa.

Per Serving: Calories: 159; Total Fat: 5g; Saturated Fat: 2g; Cholesterol: 14mg; Sodium: 398mg; Total Carbs: 21g; Dietary Fiber: 1g; Total Sugars: 1g; Protein: 6g

Curried Cauliflower With Cashews And Yogurt

Servings: 2 | Prep Time: 10 Minutes | Cooking Time: 12 Minutes

Ingredients:

- 4 cups cauliflower florets (about 340g)
- 1 tablespoon olive oil
- Salt
- 1 teaspoon curry powder
- ½ cup toasted, chopped cashews
- Cool Yogurt Drizzle:
- ¼ cup plain yogurt
- 2 tablespoons sour cream
- 1 teaspoon lemon juice
- Pinch cayenne pepper
- Salt
- 1 teaspoon honey
- 1 tablespoon chopped fresh cilantro, plus leaves for garnish

Directions:

1. Preheat air fryer to 200°C/400°F.
2. Toss cauliflower with oil, salt and curry powder to coat evenly.
3. Transfer to air fryer basket and cook for 12 mins, shaking basket a few times.
4. Make yogurt drizzle by combining all ingredients in a bowl.
5. Serve cauliflower warm with yogurt drizzle, cashews and cilantro leaves.

Variations & Ingredients Tips:

- Use Greek yogurt instead of sour cream in the drizzle.
- Add a squeeze of lime juice to the yogurt sauce.
- Sprinkle with crushed red pepper flakes for heat.

Per Serving: Calories: 265; Total Fat: 19g; Saturated Fat: 4g; Cholesterol: 10mg; Sodium: 140mg; Total Carbs: 20g; Fiber: 6g; Sugars: 8g; Protein: 8g

Latkes

Servings: 12 | Prep Time: 15 Minutes | Cooking Time: 13 Minutes

Ingredients:

- 1 russet potato
- 1/4 onion
- 2 eggs, lightly beaten
- 1/3 cup flour
- 1/2 teaspoon baking powder
- 1 teaspoon salt
- Freshly ground black pepper
- Canola or vegetable oil spray
- Chopped chives, for garnish
- Applesauce
- Sour cream

Directions:

1. Shred the potato and onion. Place in a colander and squeeze to remove excess water.
2. Transfer to a bowl and add eggs, flour, baking powder, salt and pepper. Mix to combine.
3. Shape into 1/4 cup patties and brush or spray both sides with oil.
4. Preheat air fryer to 200°C/400°F.
5. Air fry the latkes in batches for 12-13 minutes, flipping halfway, until golden brown.
6. Transfer to a platter and cover to keep warm.
7. Garnish with chopped chives and serve with apple-

sauce and sour cream.

Variations & Ingredients Tips:

- Add grated onion or garlic to the batter.
- Substitute matzo meal for half of the flour.
- Serve with smoked salmon or caviar as a topping.

Per Serving: Calories: 57; Total Fat: 0.5g; Saturated Fat: 0.1g; Cholesterol: 36mg; Sodium: 195mg; Total Carbs: 12g; Dietary Fiber: 1g; Total Sugars: 0.5g; Protein: 2g

Roast Sweet Potatoes With Parmesan

Servings: 4 | Prep Time: 10 Minutes | Cooking Time: 30 Minutes

Ingredients:

- 2 sweet potatoes, peeled and sliced
- 1/4 cup grated Parmesan
- 1 tsp olive oil
- 1 tbsp balsamic vinegar
- 1 tsp dried rosemary

Directions:

1. Preheat air fryer to 204°C/400°F.
2. Place the sweet potato slices and olive oil in a bowl and toss to coat.
3. Spritz with balsamic vinegar and sprinkle with rosemary. Toss again to coat evenly.
4. Transfer sweet potatoes to the air fryer basket in a single layer.
5. Roast for 18-25 minutes, shaking the basket at least once, until potatoes are tender.
6. Sprinkle with Parmesan cheese and serve warm.

Variations & Ingredients Tips:

- Add minced garlic or shallots to the potato coating.
- Use fresh rosemary instead of dried.
- Drizzle with honey or maple syrup before serving.

Per Serving: Calories: 366; Total Fat: 20g; Saturated Fat: 11g; Cholesterol: 89mg; Sodium: 584mg; Total Carbohydrates: 30g; Dietary Fiber: 4g; Total Sugars: 7g; Protein: 21g

Stuffed Onions

Servings: 6 | Prep Time: 15 Minutes | Cooking Time: 27 Minutes

Ingredients:

- 6 small yellow or white onions (100 to 115 g each)
- Olive oil spray
- 170 g bulk sweet Italian sausage meat (gluten-free, if a concern)
- 9 cherry tomatoes, chopped
- 3 tablespoons seasoned Italian-style dried bread crumbs (gluten-free, if a concern)
- 3 tablespoons (about 15 g) finely grated Parmesan cheese

Directions:

1. Preheat the air fryer to 165°C/325°F (or 165°C/330°F, if that's the closest setting).
2. Cut just enough off the root ends of the onions so they will stand up on a cutting board when this end is turned down. Carefully peel off just the brown, papery skin. Now cut the top quarter off each and place the onion back on the cutting board with this end facing up. Use a flatware spoon (preferably a serrated grapefruit spoon) or a melon baller to scoop out the "insides" (interior layers) of the onion, leaving enough of the bottom and side walls so that the onion does not collapse. Depending on the thickness of the layers in the onion, this may be one or two of those layers—or even three, if they're very thin.
3. Coat the insides and outsides of the onions with olive oil spray. Set the onion "shells" in the basket and air-fry for 15 minutes.
4. Meanwhile, make the filling. Set a medium skillet over medium heat for a couple of minutes, then crumble in the sausage meat. Cook, stirring often, until browned, about 4 minutes. Transfer the contents of the skillet to a medium bowl (leave the fat behind in the skillet or add it to the bowl, depending on your cross-trainer regimen). Stir in the tomatoes, bread crumbs, and cheese until well combined.
5. When the onions are ready, use a nonstick-safe spatula to gently transfer them to a cutting board. Increase the air fryer's temperature to 180°C/350°F.
6. Pack the sausage mixture into the onion shells, gently compacting the filling and mounding it up at the top.
7. When the machine is at temperature, set the onions stuffing side up in the basket with at least 6 mm between them. Air-fry for 12 minutes, or until lightly browned and sizzling hot.
8. Use a nonstick-safe spatula, and perhaps a flatware fork for balance, to transfer the onions to a cutting board or serving platter. Cool for 5 minutes before

serving.

Variations & Ingredients Tips:

- Use different types of sausage, such as spicy Italian or chicken sausage, for a variety of flavors.
- Add some chopped fresh herbs, such as parsley or basil, to the filling for extra flavor.
- For a vegetarian version, replace the sausage with cooked rice, quinoa, or lentils.

Per Serving: Calories: 140; Total Fat: 7g; Saturated Fat: 2.5g; Cholesterol: 20mg; Sodium: 270mg; Total Carbs: 11g; Fiber: 1g; Sugars: 4g; Protein: 7g

Buttered Brussels Sprouts

Servings: 4 | Prep Time: 5 Minutes | Cooking Time: 30 Minutes

Ingredients:

- ¼ cup grated Parmesan
- 2 tbsp butter, melted
- 455g Brussels sprouts
- Salt and pepper to taste

Directions:

1. Preheat air fryer to 165°C/330°F.
2. Trim the bottoms of the sprouts and remove any discolored leaves.
3. Place the sprouts in a medium bowl along with butter, salt and pepper. Toss to coat, then place them in the frying basket.
4. Roast for 20 minutes, shaking the basket twice. When done, the sprouts should be crisp with golden-brown color.
5. Plate the sprouts in a serving dish and toss with Parmesan cheese.

Variations & Ingredients Tips:

- Add crushed garlic or garlic powder to the butter mixture.
- Toss with balsamic glaze or lemon juice after cooking.
- Use olive oil instead of butter to make it vegan.

Per Serving: Calories: 130; Total Fat: 8g; Saturated Fat: 4g; Cholesterol: 15mg; Sodium: 230mg; Total Carbs: 11g; Fiber: 4g; Sugars: 3g; Protein: 6g

Beet Fries

Servings: 3 | Prep Time: 10 Minutes | Cooking Time: 22 Minutes

Ingredients:

- 3 170g red beets
- Vegetable oil spray
- To taste Coarse sea salt or kosher salt

Directions:

1. Preheat the air fryer to 190°C/375°F.
2. Remove the stems from the beets and peel them with a knife or vegetable peeler. Slice them into 1.3cm-thick circles. Lay these flat on a cutting board and slice them into 1.3cm-thick sticks. Generously coat the sticks on all sides with vegetable oil spray.
3. When the machine is at temperature, drop them into the basket, shake the basket to even the sticks out into as close to one layer as possible, and air-fry for 20 minutes, tossing and rearranging the beet matchsticks every 5 minutes, or until brown and even crisp at the ends. If the machine is at 182°C/360°F, you may need to add 2 minutes to the cooking time.
4. Pour the fries into a big bowl, add the salt, toss well, and serve warm.

Variations & Ingredients Tips:

- Toss with smoked paprika and fresh parsley after cooking.
- Add a squeeze of lemon juice and zest for brightness.
- Serve with a creamy dill or lemon aioli for dipping.

Per Serving: Calories: 70; Total Fat: 0g; Saturated Fat: 0g; Cholesterol: 0mg; Sodium: 170mg; Total Carbs: 16g; Fiber: 4g; Sugars: 11g; Protein: 3g

Famous Potato Au Gratin

Servings: 4 | Prep Time: 15 Minutes | Cooking Time: 35 Minutes

Ingredients:

- 2 russet potatoes, sliced
- ½ cup grated Gruyère cheese
- 2 tbsp Parmesan cheese
- ½ cup half-and-half
- 2 eggs
- 1 tbsp flour

- 1 garlic clove minced
- Salt and pepper to taste
- 1 tsp smoked paprika
- 1 cup diced cooked ham
- 1 tbsp butter, melted
- 1 tbsp bread crumbs
- 1 tbsp cilantro, chopped

Directions:

1. Combine the half-and-half, eggs, flour, salt, garlic, pepper, and paprika in a bowl.
2. Toss in potatoes until all sides are coated.
3. Preheat air fryer at 190°C/375°F.
4. Add half of the potato slices to a greased baking pan and pour half of the egg mixture. Top with ham and Gruyère cheese; then repeat layers.
5. Whisk the butter, Parmesan, breadcrumbs, and cilantro. Pour over casserole and cover with foil.
6. Place baking pan in fryer. Bake for 15 mins. Uncover and cook 5 more mins.
7. Let rest 10 mins before serving.

Variations & Ingredients Tips:

- Use Yukon gold potatoes instead of russet.
- Substitute cooked bacon or sausage for the ham.
- Top with crushed potato chips before baking.

Per Serving: Calories: 380; Total Fat: 20g; Saturated Fat: 10g; Cholesterol: 145mg; Sodium: 560mg; Total Carbs: 33g; Fiber: 3g; Sugars: 3g; Protein: 18g

Simple Roasted Sweet Potatoes

Servings: 2 | Prep Time: 5 Minutes | Cooking Time: 45 Minutes

Ingredients:

- 2 sweet potatoes (280 to 340 g each)

Directions:

1. Preheat the air fryer to 180°C/350°F.
2. Prick the sweet potato(es) in four or five different places with the tines of a flatware fork (not in a line but all around).
3. When the machine is at temperature, set the sweet potato(es) in the basket with as much air space between them as possible. Air-fry undisturbed for 45 minutes, or until soft when pricked with a fork.
4. Use kitchen tongs to transfer the sweet potato(es) to a wire rack. Cool for 5 minutes before serving.

Variations & Ingredients Tips:

- Serve the sweet potatoes with butter, cinnamon, or brown sugar for a sweeter flavor.
- Cut the sweet potatoes into wedges or fries for a different shape and texture.
- Try using different types of sweet potatoes, such as purple or Japanese sweet potatoes, for a unique color and flavor.

Per Serving: Calories: 180; Total Fat: 0g; Saturated Fat: 0g; Cholesterol: 0mg; Sodium: 70mg; Total Carbs: 41g; Fiber: 6g; Sugars: 13g; Protein: 4g

Thyme Sweet Potato Wedges

Servings: 4 | Prep Time: 10 Minutes | Cooking Time: 30 Minutes

Ingredients:

- 2 peeled sweet potatoes, cubed
- 30 g grated Parmesan
- 1 tablespoon olive oil
- Salt and pepper to taste
- ½ teaspoon dried thyme
- ½ teaspoon ground cumin

Directions:

1. Preheat air fryer to 165°C/330°F.
2. Add sweet potato cubes to the frying basket, then drizzle with oil. Toss to gently coat.
3. Season with salt, pepper, thyme, and cumin.
4. Roast the potatoes for about 10 minutes. Shake the basket and continue roasting for another 10 minutes.
5. Shake the basket again, this time adding Parmesan cheese. Shake and return to the air fryer.
6. Roast until the potatoes are tender, 4-6 minutes.
7. Serve and enjoy!

Variations & Ingredients Tips:

- Use different types of potatoes, such as russet or Yukon Gold, for a variety of flavors and textures.
- Add some minced garlic or red pepper flakes for extra flavor.
- Serve the sweet potato wedges with a dipping sauce, such as ranch dressing or garlic aioli.

Per Serving: Calories: 140; Total Fat: 5g; Saturated Fat: 1.5g; Cholesterol: 5mg; Sodium: 180mg; Total Carbs: 21g; Fiber: 3g; Sugars: 5g; Protein: 4g

Stunning Apples & Onions

Servings: 4 | Prep Time: 5 Minutes | Cooking Time: 30 Minutes

Ingredients:

- 2 peeled McIntosh apples, sliced
- 1 shallot, sliced
- 2 teaspoons canola oil
- 2 tablespoons brown sugar
- 1 tablespoon honey
- 1 tablespoon butter, melted
- ½ teaspoon sea salt

Directions:

1. Preheat the air fryer to 165°C/325°F.
2. Toss the shallot slices with oil in a bowl until coated. Put the bowl in the fryer and Bake for 5 minutes.
3. Remove the bowl and add the apples, brown sugar, honey, melted butter, and sea salt and stir.
4. Put the bowl back into the fryer and Bake for 10-12 more minutes or until the onions and apples are tender.
5. Stir again and serve.

Variations & Ingredients Tips:

- Use different types of apples, such as Granny Smith or Honeycrisp, for a variety of flavors and textures.
- Add some chopped nuts, such as pecans or walnuts, for a crunchy texture.
- For a savory version, replace the brown sugar and honey with balsamic vinegar and thyme.

Per Serving: Calories: 140; Total Fat: 5g; Saturated Fat: 2g; Cholesterol: 10mg; Sodium: 300mg; Total Carbs: 25g; Fiber: 2g; Sugars: 20g; Protein: 0g

Fried Corn On The Cob

Servings: 2 | Prep Time: 10 Minutes | Cooking Time: 10 Minutes

Ingredients:

- 1½ tablespoons Regular or low-fat mayonnaise
- 1½ teaspoons Minced garlic
- ¼ teaspoon Table salt
- ¾ cup Plain panko bread crumbs
- 3 10cm lengths husked and de-silked corn on the cob
- Vegetable oil spray

Directions:

1. Preheat air fryer to 200°C/400°F.
2. Stir mayo, garlic, salt. Spread panko on a plate.
3. Brush mayo mix over corn kernels. Roll in panko to coat.
4. Spray corn with oil. Set aside and coat remaining pieces.
5. Set coated corn in basket with space between. Air fry 10 mins until crisp.
6. Transfer to wire rack. Cool 5 mins before serving.

Variations & Ingredients Tips:

- Use chipotle mayo for a smoky flavor.
- Add parmesan or cajun seasoning to the breadcrumb coating.
- Serve with lime wedges for squeezing over.

Per Serving: Calories: 210; Total Fat: 8g; Saturated Fat: 1g; Cholesterol: 5mg; Sodium: 440mg; Total Carbs: 31g; Fiber: 3g; Sugars: 3g; Protein: 6g

Herbed Baby Red Potato Hasselback

Servings: 4 | Prep Time: 10 Minutes | Cooking Time: 35 Minutes

Ingredients:

- 6 baby red potatoes, scrubbed
- 3 tsp shredded cheddar cheese
- 1 tbsp olive oil
- 2 tbsp butter, melted
- 1 tbsp chopped thyme
- Salt and pepper to taste
- 3 tsp sour cream
- 1/4 cup chopped parsley

Directions:

1. Preheat air fryer at 180°C/350°F.
2. Make slices in the width of each potato about 6mm apart without cutting through.
3. Rub potato slices with olive oil, both outside and in between slices.
4. Place potatoes in the frying basket and air fry for 20 minutes, tossing once.
5. Brush with melted butter, and scatter with thyme.
6. Remove them to a large serving dish. Sprinkle with salt, black pepper and top with a dollop of cheddar

cheese, sour cream.
7. Scatter with parsley to serve.

Variations & Ingredients Tips:

- Use fresh rosemary or oregano instead of thyme.
- Mix cheese into melted butter before brushing on potatoes.
- Serve with ranch or blue cheese dressing for dipping.

Per Serving: Calories: 217; Total Fat: 14g; Saturated Fat: 6g; Cholesterol: 23mg; Sodium: 133mg; Total Carbs: 20g; Dietary Fiber: 3g; Total Sugars: 2g; Protein: 4g

Parmesan Asparagus

Servings: 2 | Prep Time: 5 Minutes | Cooking Time: 5 Minutes

Ingredients:

- 1 bunch asparagus, stems trimmed
- 1 teaspoon olive oil
- Salt and freshly ground black pepper
- 1/4 cup coarsely grated Parmesan cheese
- 1/2 lemon

Directions:

1. Preheat the air fryer to 200°C/400°F.
2. Toss the asparagus with the oil and season with salt and pepper.
3. Transfer asparagus to the air fryer basket and cook at 204°C/400°F for 5 minutes, shaking basket once or twice.
4. When asparagus is cooked, sprinkle with Parmesan cheese and close air fryer drawer. Let sit for 1 minute.
5. Remove asparagus, transfer to a dish and finish with black pepper and a squeeze of lemon juice.

Variations & Ingredients Tips:

- Add garlic powder or red pepper flakes for extra flavor.
- Use lemon zest instead of juice for more intense lemon flavor.
- Drizzle with balsamic glaze or melted butter before serving.

Per Serving: Calories: 81; Total Fat: 5g; Saturated Fat: 2g; Cholesterol: 7mg; Sodium: 147mg; Total Carbohydrates: 6g; Dietary Fiber: 3g; Total Sugars: 3g; Protein: 5g

Roasted Garlic And Thyme Tomatoes

Servings: 2 | Prep Time: 5 Minutes | Cooking Time: 15 Minutes

Ingredients:

- 4 Roma tomatoes
- 1 tablespoon olive oil
- Salt and freshly ground black pepper
- 1 clove garlic, minced
- 1/2 teaspoon dried thyme

Directions:

1. Preheat air fryer to 199°C/390°F.
2. Cut tomatoes in half and scoop out seeds/pithy parts.
3. In a bowl, toss tomatoes with olive oil, salt, pepper, garlic and thyme.
4. Transfer tomatoes cut-side up to air fryer basket.
5. Air fry for 15 minutes until edges just start to brown.
6. Let cool slightly before serving.

Variations & Ingredients Tips:

- Use cherry or grape tomatoes instead of Roma.
- Add balsamic vinegar or red pepper flakes for extra flavor.
- Top with grated parmesan or mozzarella before serving.

Per Serving: Calories: 71; Total Fat: 5g; Saturated Fat: 1g; Cholesterol: 0mg; Sodium: 7mg; Total Carbohydrates: 6g; Dietary Fiber: 2g; Total Sugars: 4g; Protein: 1g

Sandwiches And Burgers Recipes

Chicken Saltimbocca Sandwiches

Servings: 3 | Prep Time: 10 Minutes | Cooking Time: 11 Minutes

Ingredients:

- 3 140to 170-gram boneless skinless chicken breasts
- 6 Thin prosciutto slices
- 6 Provolone cheese slices
- 3 Long soft rolls, such as hero, hoagie, or Italian sub rolls (gluten-free, if a concern), split open lengthwise
- 3 tablespoons Pesto, purchased or homemade (see the headnote)

Directions:

1. Preheat the air fryer to 200°C/400°F.
2. Wrap each chicken breast with 2 prosciutto slices, spiraling the prosciutto around the breast and overlapping the slices a bit to cover the breast. The prosciutto will stick to the chicken more readily than bacon does.
3. When the machine is at temperature, set the wrapped chicken breasts in the basket and air-fry undisturbed for 10 minutes, or until the prosciutto is frizzled and the chicken is cooked through.
4. Overlap 2 cheese slices on each breast. Air-fry undisturbed for 1 minute, or until melted. Take the basket out of the machine.
5. Smear the insides of the rolls with the pesto, then use kitchen tongs to put a wrapped and cheesy chicken breast in each roll.

Variations & Ingredients Tips:

- Use fresh mozzarella instead of provolone for a creamier texture.
- Add sliced tomatoes or roasted red peppers for extra flavor and nutrition.
- Substitute prosciutto with ham or bacon if desired.

Per Serving: Calories: 630; Cholesterol: 125mg; Total Fat: 32g; Saturated Fat: 11g; Sodium: 1580mg; Total Carbohydrates: 38g; Dietary Fiber: 2g; Total Sugars: 4g; Protein: 48g

Inside-out Cheeseburgers

Servings: 3 | Prep Time: 15 Minutes | Cooking Time: 9-11 Minutes

Ingredients:

- 510 grams 90% lean ground beef
- ¾ teaspoon Dried oregano
- ¾ teaspoon Table salt
- ¾ teaspoon Ground black pepper
- ¼ teaspoon Garlic powder
- 6 tablespoons (about 45 grams) Shredded Cheddar, Swiss, or other semi-firm cheese, or a purchased blend of shredded cheeses
- 3 Hamburger buns (gluten-free, if a concern), split open

Directions:

1. Preheat the air fryer to 190°C/375°F.
2. Gently mix the ground beef, oregano, salt, pepper, and garlic powder in a bowl until well combined without turning the mixture to mush. Form it into two 15-cm patties for the small batch, three for the medium, or four for the large.
3. Place 2 tablespoons of the shredded cheese in the center of each patty. With clean hands, fold the sides of the patty up to cover the cheese, then pick it up and roll it gently into a ball to seal the cheese inside. Gently press it back into a 12.5-cm burger without letting any cheese squish out. Continue filling and preparing more burgers, as needed.
4. Place the burgers in the basket in one layer and air-fry undisturbed for 8 minutes for medium or 10 minutes for well-done. (An instant-read meat thermometer won't work for these burgers because it will hit the mostly melted cheese inside and offer a hotter temperature than the surrounding meat.)
5. Use a nonstick-safe spatula, and perhaps a flatware

fork for balance, to transfer the burgers to a cutting board. Set the buns cut side down in the basket in one layer (working in batches as necessary) and air-fry undisturbed for 1 minute, to toast a bit and warm up. Cool the burgers a few minutes more, then serve them warm in the buns.

Variations & Ingredients Tips:

- Mix different types of cheese like cheddar, mozzarella, and blue cheese for a flavorful combination.
- Add finely chopped bacon or caramelized onions to the cheese stuffing for extra richness.
- Serve with your favorite burger toppings like lettuce, tomato, onion, and pickles.

Per Serving (1 burger): Calories: 480; Cholesterol: 125mg; Total Fat: 27g; Saturated Fat: 11g; Sodium: 720mg; Total Carbohydrates: 22g; Dietary Fiber: 1g; Total Sugars: 3g; Protein: 38g

Thanksgiving Turkey Sandwiches

Servings: 3 | Prep Time: 15 Minutes | Cooking Time: 10 Minutes

Ingredients:

- 1½ cups Herb-seasoned stuffing mix (not cornbread-style; gluten-free, if a concern)
- 1 Large egg white(s)
- 2 tablespoons Water
- 3 140- to 170-gram turkey breast cutlets
- Vegetable oil spray
- 4½ tablespoons Purchased cranberry sauce, preferably whole berry
- ⅛ teaspoon Ground cinnamon
- ⅛ teaspoon Ground dried ginger
- 4½ tablespoons Regular, low-fat, or fat-free mayonnaise (gluten-free, if a concern)
- 6 tablespoons Shredded Brussels sprouts
- 3 Kaiser rolls (gluten-free, if a concern), split open

Directions:

1. Preheat the air fryer to 190°C/375°F.
2. Put the stuffing mix in a heavy zip-closed bag, seal it, lay it flat on your counter, and roll a rolling pin over the bag to crush the stuffing mix to the consistency of rough sand. (Or you can pulse the stuffing mix to the desired consistency in a food processor.)
3. Set up and fill two shallow soup plates or small pie plates on your counter: one for the egg white(s), whisked with the water until foamy; and one for the ground stuffing mix.
4. Dip a cutlet in the egg white mixture, coating both sides and letting any excess egg white slip back into the rest. Set the cutlet in the ground stuffing mix and coat it evenly on both sides, pressing gently to coat well on both sides. Lightly coat the cutlet on both sides with vegetable oil spray, set it aside, and continue dipping and coating the remaining cutlets in the same way.
5. Set the cutlets in the basket and air-fry undisturbed for 10 minutes, or until crisp and brown. Use kitchen tongs to transfer the cutlets to a wire rack to cool for a few minutes.
6. Meanwhile, stir the cranberry sauce with the cinnamon and ginger in a small bowl. Mix the shredded Brussels sprouts and mayonnaise in a second bowl until the vegetable is evenly coated.
7. Build the sandwiches by spreading about 1½ tablespoons of the cranberry mixture on the cut side of the bottom half of each roll. Set a cutlet on top, then spread about 3 tablespoons of the Brussels sprouts mixture evenly over the cutlet. Set the other half of the roll on top and serve warm.

Variations & Ingredients Tips:

- Use leftover roasted turkey instead of turkey cutlets for a post-Thanksgiving sandwich.
- Substitute Brussels sprouts with shredded cabbage or kale for a different texture and flavor.
- Add a slice of brie or provolone cheese to the sandwich for extra creaminess.

Per Serving: Calories: 530; Cholesterol: 75mg; Total Fat: 22g; Saturated Fat: 4g; Sodium: 1180mg; Total Carbohydrates: 53g; Dietary Fiber: 4g; Total Sugars: 15g; Protein: 33g

Black Bean Veggie Burgers

Servings: 3 | Prep Time: 15 Minutes | Cooking Time: 10 Minutes

Ingredients:

- 1 cup Drained and rinsed canned black beans
- ⅓ cup Pecan pieces
- ⅓ cup Rolled oats (not quick-cooking or steel-cut; gluten-free, if a concern)
- 2 tablespoons (or 1 small egg) Pasteurized egg substitute, such as Egg Beaters (gluten-free, if a concern)
- 2 teaspoons Red ketchup-like chili sauce, such

- as Heinz
- ¼ teaspoon Ground cumin
- ¼ teaspoon Dried oregano
- ¼ teaspoon Table salt
- ¼ teaspoon Ground black pepper
- Olive oil
- Olive oil spray

Directions:

1. Preheat the air fryer to 200°C/400°F.
2. Put the beans, pecans, oats, egg substitute or egg, chili sauce, cumin, oregano, salt, and pepper in a food processor. Cover and process to a coarse paste that will hold its shape like sugar-cookie dough, adding olive oil in 1-teaspoon increments to get the mixture to blend smoothly. The amount of olive oil is actually dependent on the internal moisture content of the beans and the oats. Figure on about 1 tablespoon (three 1-teaspoon additions) for the smaller batch, with proportional increases for the other batches. A little too much olive oil can't hurt, but a dry paste will fall apart as it cooks and a far-too-wet paste will stick to the basket.
3. Scrape down and remove the blade. Using clean, wet hands, form the paste into two 10 cm patties for the small batch, three 10 cm patties for the medium, or four 10 cm patties for the large batch, setting them one by one on a cutting board. Generously coat both sides of the patties with olive oil spray.
4. Set them in the basket in one layer. Air-fry undisturbed for 10 minutes, or until lightly browned and crisp at the edges.
5. Use a nonstick-safe spatula, and perhaps a flatware fork for balance, to transfer the burgers to a wire rack. Cool for 5 minutes before serving.

Variations & Ingredients Tips:

- Add finely chopped vegetables like bell peppers, onions, or carrots for extra flavor and nutrition.
- Experiment with different spices and herbs, such as smoked paprika, garlic powder, or cilantro.
- For a gluten-free version, ensure all ingredients are certified gluten-free.

Per Serving: Calories: 280; Cholesterol: 0mg; Total Fat: 15g; Saturated Fat: 2g; Sodium: 420mg; Total Carbohydrates: 28g; Dietary Fiber: 8g; Total Sugars: 2g; Protein: 10g

Asian Glazed Meatballs

Servings: 4 | Prep Time: 15 Minutes | Cooking Time: 10 Minutes

Ingredients:

- 1 large shallot, finely chopped
- 2 cloves garlic, minced
- 1 tablespoon grated fresh ginger
- 2 teaspoons fresh thyme, finely chopped
- 1½ cups brown mushrooms, very finely chopped (a food processor works well here)
- 2 tablespoons soy sauce
- freshly ground black pepper
- ½ kg ground beef
- ¼ kg ground pork
- 3 egg yolks
- 1 cup Thai sweet chili sauce (spring roll sauce)
- ¼ cup toasted sesame seeds
- 2 scallions, sliced

Directions:

1. Combine the shallot, garlic, ginger, thyme, mushrooms, soy sauce, freshly ground black pepper, ground beef and pork, and egg yolks in a bowl and mix the ingredients together. Gently shape the mixture into 24 balls, about the size of a golf ball.
2. Preheat the air fryer to 190°C/380°F.
3. Working in batches, air-fry the meatballs for 8 minutes, turning the meatballs over halfway through the cooking time. Drizzle some of the Thai sweet chili sauce on top of each meatball and return the basket to the air fryer, air-frying for another 2 minutes. Reserve the remaining Thai sweet chili sauce for serving.
4. As soon as the meatballs are done, sprinkle with toasted sesame seeds and transfer them to a serving platter. Scatter the scallions around and serve warm.

Variations & Ingredients Tips:

- Use a food processor to finely chop the mushrooms for better texture in the meatballs.
- Work in batches when air frying the meatballs to ensure even cooking and browning.
- Drizzle the Thai sweet chili sauce over the meatballs towards the end of cooking for a nice glaze.

Per Serving: Calories: 550; Cholesterol: 205mg; Total Fat: 32g; Saturated Fat: 11g; Sodium: 1300mg; Total Carbohydrates: 36g; Dietary Fiber: 2g; Total Sugars: 23g; Protein: 29g

Chicken Club Sandwiches

Servings: 3 | Prep Time: 15 Minutes | Cooking Time: 15 Minutes

Ingredients:

- 3 140- to 170-gram boneless skinless chicken breasts
- 6 Thick-cut bacon strips (gluten-free, if a concern)
- 3 Long soft rolls, such as hero, hoagie, or Italian sub rolls (gluten-free, if a concern)
- 3 tablespoons Regular, low-fat, or fat-free mayonnaise (gluten-free, if a concern)
- 3 Lettuce leaves, preferably romaine or iceberg
- 6 6-mm-thick tomato slices

Directions:

1. Preheat the air fryer to 190°C/375°F.
2. Wrap each chicken breast with 2 strips of bacon, spiraling the bacon around the meat, slightly overlapping the strips on each revolution. Start the second strip of bacon farther down the breast but on a line with the start of the first strip so they both end at a lined-up point on the chicken breast.
3. When the machine is at temperature, set the wrapped breasts bacon-seam side down in the basket with space between them. Air-fry undisturbed for 12 minutes, until the bacon is browned, crisp, and cooked through and an instant-read meat thermometer inserted into the center of a breast registers 75°C/165°F. You may need to add 2 minutes in the air fryer if the temperature is at 70°C/160°F.
4. Use kitchen tongs to transfer the breasts to a wire rack. Split the rolls open lengthwise and set them cut side down in the basket. Air-fry for 1 minute, or until warmed through.
5. Use kitchen tongs to transfer the rolls to a cutting board. Spread 1 tablespoon mayonnaise on the cut side of one half of each roll. Top with a chicken breast, lettuce leaf, and tomato slice. Serve warm.

Variations & Ingredients Tips:

- Use turkey bacon for a lower-fat option.
- Add sliced avocado or pickled onions for extra flavor and texture.
- Toast the rolls before assembling the sandwiches for a crispy texture.

Per Serving: Calories: 640; Cholesterol: 110mg; Total Fat: 34g; Saturated Fat: 9g; Sodium: 1180mg; Total Carbohydrates: 44g; Dietary Fiber: 2g; Total Sugars: 5g; Protein: 42g

Thai-style Pork Sliders

Servings: 4 | Prep Time: 15 Minutes | Cooking Time: 15 Minutes

Ingredients:

- 310 grams Ground pork
- 2½ tablespoons Very thinly sliced scallions, white and green parts
- 4 teaspoons Minced peeled fresh ginger
- 2½ teaspoons Fish sauce (gluten-free, if a concern)
- 2 teaspoons Thai curry paste (see the headnote; gluten-free, if a concern)
- 2 teaspoons Light brown sugar
- ¾ teaspoon Ground black pepper
- 4 Slider buns (gluten-free, if a concern)

Directions:

1. Preheat the air fryer to 190°C/375°F.
2. Gently mix the pork, scallions, ginger, fish sauce, curry paste, brown sugar, and black pepper in a bowl until well combined. With clean, wet hands, form about 80 grams of the pork mixture into a slider about 6.5-cm in diameter. Repeat until you use up all the meat—3 sliders for the small batch, 4 for the medium, and 6 for the large. (Keep wetting your hands to help the patties adhere.)
3. When the machine is at temperature, set the sliders in the basket in one layer. Air-fry undisturbed for 14 minutes, or until the sliders are golden brown and caramelized at their edges and an instant-read meat thermometer inserted into the center of a slider registers 70°C/160°F.
4. Use a nonstick-safe spatula, and perhaps a flatware fork for balance, to transfer the sliders to a cutting board. Set the buns cut side down in the basket in one layer (working in batches as necessary) and air-fry undisturbed for 1 minute, to toast a bit and warm up. Serve the sliders warm in the buns.

Variations & Ingredients Tips:

- Use ground chicken or turkey for a leaner slider option.
- Substitute Thai curry paste with red curry paste or green curry paste for a different flavor profile.

- Serve with pickled vegetables, cilantro, and sriracha mayonnaise for extra Thai-inspired toppings.

Per Serving (1 slider): Calories: 240; Cholesterol: 65mg; Total Fat: 13g; Saturated Fat: 4g; Sodium: 490mg; Total Carbohydrates: 18g; Dietary Fiber: 1g; Total Sugars: 4g; Protein: 15g

Chicken Spiedies

Servings: 3 | Prep Time: 15 Minutes (plus Marinating Time) | Cooking Time: 12 Minutes

Ingredients:

- 570 grams Boneless skinless chicken thighs, trimmed of any fat blobs and cut into 5-cm pieces
- 3 tablespoons Red wine vinegar
- 2 tablespoons Olive oil
- 2 tablespoons Minced fresh mint leaves
- 2 tablespoons Minced fresh parsley leaves
- 2 teaspoons Minced fresh dill fronds
- ¾ teaspoon Fennel seeds
- ¾ teaspoon Table salt
- Up to a ¼ teaspoon Red pepper flakes
- 3 Long soft rolls, such as hero, hoagie, or Italian sub rolls (gluten-free, if a concern), split open lengthwise
- 4½ tablespoons Regular or low-fat mayonnaise (not fat-free; gluten-free, if a concern)
- 1½ tablespoons Distilled white vinegar
- 1½ teaspoons Ground black pepper

Directions:

1. Mix the chicken, vinegar, oil, mint, parsley, dill, fennel seeds, salt, and red pepper flakes in a zip-closed plastic bag. Seal, gently massage the marinade ingredients into the meat, and refrigerate for at least 2 hours or up to 6 hours. (Longer than that and the meat can turn rubbery.)
2. Set the plastic bag out on the counter (to make the contents a little less frigid). Preheat the air fryer to 200°C/400°F.
3. When the machine is at temperature, use kitchen tongs to set the chicken thighs in the basket (discard any remaining marinade) and air-fry undisturbed for 6 minutes. Turn the thighs over and continue air-frying undisturbed for 6 minutes more, until well browned, cooked through, and even a little crunchy.
4. Dump the contents of the basket onto a wire rack and cool for 2 or 3 minutes. Divide the chicken evenly between the rolls. Whisk the mayonnaise, vinegar, and black pepper in a small bowl until smooth. Drizzle this sauce over the chicken pieces in the rolls.

Variations & Ingredients Tips:

- Use chicken breast instead of thighs for a leaner option.
- Substitute the herbs with your favorite combination, such as basil, oregano, or thyme.
- Add sliced onions or pickled vegetables for extra crunch and tanginess.

Per Serving: Calories: 710; Cholesterol: 200mg; Total Fat: 44g; Saturated Fat: 8g; Sodium: 1240mg; Total Carbohydrates: 37g; Dietary Fiber: 2g; Total Sugars: 4g; Protein: 45g

Sausage And Pepper Heros

Servings: 3 | Prep Time: 10 Minutes | Cooking Time: 11 Minutes

Ingredients:

- 3 links (about 255 grams total) Sweet Italian sausages (gluten-free, if a concern)
- 1½ Medium red or green bell pepper(s), stemmed, cored, and cut into 1.25-cm-wide strips
- 1 medium Yellow or white onion(s), peeled, halved, and sliced into thin half-moons
- 3 Long soft rolls, such as hero, hoagie, or Italian sub rolls (gluten-free, if a concern), split open lengthwise
- For garnishing Balsamic vinegar
- For garnishing Fresh basil leaves

Directions:

1. Preheat the air fryer to 200°C/400°F.
2. When the machine is at temperature, set the sausage links in the basket in one layer and air-fry undisturbed for 5 minutes.
3. Add the pepper strips and onions. Continue air-frying, tossing and rearranging everything about once every minute, for 5 minutes, or until the sausages are browned and an instant-read meat thermometer inserted into one of the links registers 70°C/160°F.
4. Use a nonstick-safe spatula and kitchen tongs to transfer the sausages and vegetables to a cutting board. Set the rolls cut side down in the basket in one layer (working in batches as necessary) and air-fry undisturbed for 1 minute, to toast the rolls a bit and warm

them up. Set 1 sausage with some pepper strips and onions in each warm roll, sprinkle balsamic vinegar over the sandwich fillings, and garnish with basil leaves.

Variations & Ingredients Tips:

- Use hot Italian sausage or chorizo for a spicier sandwich.
- Add sliced mushrooms or zucchini to the pepper and onion mixture for extra veggies.
- Top with shredded mozzarella or provolone cheese for a cheesy twist.

Per Serving (1 sandwich): Calories: 560; Cholesterol: 60mg; Total Fat: 36g; Saturated Fat: 12g; Sodium: 1420mg; Total Carbohydrates: 39g; Dietary Fiber: 3g; Total Sugars: 7g; Protein: 24g

Crunchy Falafel Balls

Servings: 8 | Prep Time: 15 Minutes | Cooking Time: 16 Minutes

Ingredients:

- 600 grams Drained and rinsed canned chickpeas
- 60 grams Olive oil
- 3 tablespoons All-purpose flour
- 1½ teaspoons Dried oregano
- 1½ teaspoons Dried sage leaves
- 1½ teaspoons Dried thyme
- ¾ teaspoon Table salt
- Olive oil spray

Directions:

1. Preheat the air fryer to 200°C/400°F.
2. Place the chickpeas, olive oil, flour, oregano, sage, thyme, and salt in a food processor. Cover and process into a paste, stopping the machine at least once to scrape down the inside of the canister.
3. Scrape down and remove the blade. Using clean, wet hands, form 2 tablespoons of the paste into a ball, then continue making 9 more balls for a small batch, 15 more for a medium one, and 19 more for a large batch. Generously coat the balls in olive oil spray.
4. Set the balls in the basket in one layer with a little space between them and air-fry undisturbed for 16 minutes, or until well browned and crisp.
5. Dump the contents of the basket onto a wire rack. Cool for 5 minutes before serving.

Variations & Ingredients Tips:

- Add minced garlic, onion, or herbs like parsley or cilantro for extra flavor.
- Serve with tahini sauce, hummus, or tzatziki for dipping.
- Make a falafel sandwich by stuffing pita bread with falafel balls, lettuce, tomato, and sauce.

Per Serving (2 falafel balls): Calories: 170; Cholesterol: 0mg; Total Fat: 9g; Saturated Fat: 1g; Sodium: 230mg; Total Carbohydrates: 18g; Dietary Fiber: 4g; Total Sugars: 2g; Protein: 5g

Salmon Burgers

Servings: 3 | Prep Time: 15 Minutes | Cooking Time: 8 Minutes

Ingredients:

- 510 grams Skinless salmon fillet, preferably fattier Atlantic salmon
- 1½ tablespoons Minced chives or the green part of a scallion
- ½ cup Plain panko bread crumbs (gluten-free, if a concern)
- 1½ teaspoons Dijon mustard (gluten-free, if a concern)
- 1½ teaspoons Drained and rinsed capers, minced
- 1½ teaspoons Lemon juice
- ¼ teaspoon Table salt
- ¼ teaspoon Ground black pepper
- Vegetable oil spray

Directions:

1. Preheat the air fryer to 190°C/375°F.
2. Cut the salmon into pieces that will fit in a food processor. Cover and pulse until coarsely chopped. Add the chives and pulse to combine, until the fish is ground but not a paste. Scrape down and remove the blade. Scrape the salmon mixture into a bowl. Add the bread crumbs, mustard, capers, lemon juice, salt, and pepper. Stir gently until well combined.
3. Use clean and dry hands to form the mixture into two 12.5-cm patties for a small batch, three 12.5-cm patties for a medium batch, or four 12.5-cm patties for a large one.
4. Coat both sides of each patty with vegetable oil spray. Set them in the basket in one layer and air-fry undisturbed for 8 minutes, or until browned and an in-

stant-read meat thermometer inserted into the center of a burger registers 65°C/145°F.
5. Use a nonstick-safe spatula, and perhaps a flatware fork for balance, to transfer the burgers to a wire rack. Cool for 2 or 3 minutes before serving.

Variations & Ingredients Tips:

- Substitute salmon with canned or leftover cooked salmon for convenience.
- Add finely chopped red bell pepper or celery to the burger mixture for extra crunch and flavor.
- Serve on toasted buns with lettuce, tomato, and a dollop of tartar sauce or remoulade.

Per Serving (1 burger): Calories: 320; Cholesterol: 95mg; Total Fat: 16g; Saturated Fat: 3g; Sodium: 440mg; Total Carbohydrates: 15g; Dietary Fiber: 1g; Total Sugars: 1g; Protein: 31g

Dijon Thyme Burgers

Servings: 3 | Prep Time: 15 Minutes | Cooking Time: 18 Minutes

Ingredients:

- 450 grams lean ground beef
- ⅓ cup panko breadcrumbs
- ¼ cup finely chopped onion
- 3 tablespoons Dijon mustard
- 1 tablespoon chopped fresh thyme
- 4 teaspoons Worcestershire sauce
- 1 teaspoon salt
- freshly ground black pepper
- Topping (optional):
- 2 tablespoons Dijon mustard
- 1 tablespoon dark brown sugar
- 1 teaspoon Worcestershire sauce
- 115 grams sliced Swiss cheese, optional

Directions:

1. Combine all the burger ingredients together in a large bowl and mix well. Divide the meat into 4 equal portions and then form the burgers, being careful not to over-handle the meat. One good way to do this is to throw the meat back and forth from one hand to another, packing the meat each time you catch it. Flatten the balls into patties, making an indentation in the center of each patty with your thumb (this will help it stay flat as it cooks) and flattening the sides of the burgers so that they will fit nicely into the air fryer basket.
2. Preheat the air fryer to 190°C/370°F.
3. If you don't have room for all four burgers, air-fry two or three burgers at a time for 8 minutes. Flip the burgers over and air-fry for another 6 minutes.
4. While the burgers are cooking combine the Dijon mustard, dark brown sugar, and Worcestershire sauce in a small bowl and mix well. This optional topping to the burgers really adds a boost of flavor at the end. Spread the Dijon topping evenly on each burger. If you cooked the burgers in batches, return the first batch to the cooker at this time – it's ok to place the fourth burger on top of the others in the center of the basket. Air-fry the burgers for another 3 minutes.
5. Finally, if desired, top each burger with a slice of Swiss cheese. Lower the air fryer temperature to 165°C/330°F and air-fry for another minute to melt the cheese. Serve the burgers on toasted brioche buns, dressed the way you like them.

Variations & Ingredients Tips:

- Use ground turkey or chicken for a leaner burger option.
- Add minced garlic or finely chopped herbs like parsley or chives for extra flavor.
- Substitute panko breadcrumbs with regular breadcrumbs or oats for a different texture.

Per Serving (1 burger with cheese): Calories: 500; Cholesterol: 120mg; Total Fat: 27g; Saturated Fat: 11g; Sodium: 1180mg; Total Carbohydrates: 21g; Dietary Fiber: 1g; Total Sugars: 5g; Protein: 41g

Inside Out Cheeseburgers

Servings: 2 | Prep Time: 15 Minutes | Cooking Time: 20 Minutes

Ingredients:

- 340 grams lean ground beef
- 3 tablespoons minced onion
- 4 teaspoons ketchup
- 2 teaspoons yellow mustard
- salt and freshly ground black pepper
- 4 slices of Cheddar cheese, broken into smaller pieces
- 8 hamburger dill pickle chips

Directions:

1. Combine the ground beef, minced onion, ketchup, mustard, salt and pepper in a large bowl. Mix well to thoroughly combine the ingredients. Divide the meat into four equal portions.

2. To make the stuffed burgers, flatten each portion of meat into a thin patty. Place 4 pickle chips and half of the cheese onto the center of two of the patties, leaving a rim around the edge of the patty exposed. Place the remaining two patties on top of the first and press the meat together firmly, sealing the edges tightly. With the burgers on a flat surface, press the sides of the burger with the palm of your hand to create a straight edge. This will help keep the stuffing inside the burger while it cooks.
3. Preheat the air fryer to 190°C/370°F.
4. Place the burgers inside the air fryer basket and air-fry for 20 minutes, flipping the burgers over halfway through the cooking time.
5. Serve the cheeseburgers on buns with lettuce and tomato.

Variations & Ingredients Tips:

- Use different types of cheese like Swiss, pepper jack, or blue cheese for a unique flavor.
- Add crispy bacon pieces or sautéed mushrooms to the stuffing for extra richness.
- Brush the burgers with a mixture of melted butter and minced garlic before cooking for added flavor.

Per Serving (1 burger): Calories: 510; Cholesterol: 145mg; Total Fat: 32g; Saturated Fat: 14g; Sodium: 780mg; Total Carbohydrates: 12g; Dietary Fiber: 1g; Total Sugars: 6g; Protein: 42g

Eggplant Parmesan Subs

Servings: 2 | Prep Time: 10 Minutes | Cooking Time: 13 Minutes

Ingredients:

- 4 Peeled eggplant slices (about 1.25 cm thick and 7.5 cm in diameter)
- Olive oil spray
- 2 tablespoons plus 2 teaspoons Jarred pizza sauce, any variety except creamy
- ¼ cup (about 20 grams) Finely grated Parmesan cheese
- 2 Small, long soft rolls, such as hero, hoagie, or Italian sub rolls (gluten-free, if a concern), split open lengthwise

Directions:

1. Preheat the air fryer to 175°C/350°F.
2. When the machine is at temperature, coat both sides of the eggplant slices with olive oil spray. Set them in the basket in one layer and air-fry undisturbed for 10 minutes, until lightly browned and softened.
3. Increase the machine's temperature to 190°C/375°F (or 185°C/370°F, if that's the closest setting—unless the machine is already at 180°C/360°F, in which case leave it alone). Top each eggplant slice with 2 teaspoons pizza sauce, then 1 tablespoon of cheese. Air-fry undisturbed for 2 minutes, or until the cheese has melted.
4. Use a nonstick-safe spatula, and perhaps a flatware fork for balance, to transfer the eggplant slices cheese side up to a cutting board. Set the roll(s) cut side down in the basket in one layer (working in batches as necessary) and air-fry undisturbed for 1 minute, to toast the rolls a bit and warm them up. Set 2 eggplant slices in each warm roll.

Variations & Ingredients Tips:

- Use zucchini slices instead of eggplant for a different vegetable option.
- Add a slice of fresh mozzarella on top of the Parmesan for extra cheesiness.
- Sprinkle some dried herbs like oregano or basil on the eggplant before cooking for extra flavor.

Per Serving (1 sandwich): Calories: 280; Cholesterol: 10mg; Total Fat: 9g; Saturated Fat: 3g; Sodium: 840mg; Total Carbohydrates: 40g; Dietary Fiber: 5g; Total Sugars: 8g; Protein: 11g

Chili Cheese Dogs

Servings: 3 | Prep Time: 10 Minutes | Cooking Time: 12 Minutes

Ingredients:

- 340 grams Lean ground beef
- 1½ tablespoons Chile powder
- 240 grams plus 2 tablespoons Jarred sofrito
- 3 Hot dogs (gluten-free, if a concern)
- 3 Hot dog buns (gluten-free, if a concern), split open lengthwise
- 3 tablespoons Finely chopped scallion
- 60 grams Shredded Cheddar cheese

Directions:

1. Crumble the ground beef into a medium or large saucepan set over medium heat. Brown well, stirring often to break up the clumps. Add the chile powder and cook for 30 seconds, stirring the whole time. Stir in the sofrito and bring to a simmer. Reduce the heat to low

and simmer, stirring occasionally, for 5 minutes. Keep warm.
2. Preheat the air fryer to 200°C/400°F.
3. When the machine is at temperature, put the hot dogs in the basket and air-fry undisturbed for 10 minutes, or until the hot dogs are bubbling and blistered, even a little crisp.
4. Use kitchen tongs to put the hot dogs in the buns. Top each with about 120 grams of the ground beef mixture, 1 tablespoon of the minced scallion, and 20 grams of the cheese. (The scallion should go under the cheese so it superheats and wilts a bit.) Set the filled hot dog buns in the basket and air-fry undisturbed for 2 minutes, or until the cheese has melted.
5. Remove the basket from the machine. Cool the chili cheese dogs in the basket for 5 minutes before serving.

Variations & Ingredients Tips:

- Use turkey or veggie hot dogs for a healthier option.
- Substitute cheddar cheese with your favorite melty cheese, such as pepper jack or Swiss.
- Add diced onions or jalapeños to the chili for extra flavor and heat.

Per Serving: Calories: 580; Cholesterol: 110mg; Total Fat: 32g; Saturated Fat: 13g; Sodium: 1420mg; Total Carbohydrates: 36g; Dietary Fiber: 5g; Total Sugars: 6g; Protein: 38g

Reuben Sandwiches

Servings: 2 | Prep Time: 10 Minutes | Cooking Time: 11 Minutes

Ingredients:

- 225 grams Sliced deli corned beef
- 4 teaspoons Regular or low-fat mayonnaise (not fat-free)
- 4 Rye bread slices
- 2 tablespoons plus 2 teaspoons Russian dressing
- ½ cup Purchased sauerkraut, squeezed by the handful over the sink to get rid of excess moisture
- 55 grams (2 to 4 slices) Swiss cheese slices (optional)

Directions:

1. Set the corned beef in the basket, slip the basket into the machine, and heat the air fryer to 200°C/400°F. Air-fry undisturbed for 3 minutes from the time the basket is put in the machine, just to warm up the meat.
2. Use kitchen tongs to transfer the corned beef to a cutting board. Spread 1 teaspoon mayonnaise on one side of each slice of rye bread, rubbing the mayonnaise into the bread with a small flatware knife.
3. Place the bread slices mayonnaise side down on a cutting board. Spread the Russian dressing over the "dry" side of each slice. For one sandwich, top one slice of bread with the corned beef, sauerkraut, and cheese (if using). For two sandwiches, top two slices of bread each with half of the corned beef, sauerkraut, and cheese (if using). Close the sandwiches with the remaining bread, setting it mayonnaise side up on top.
4. Set the sandwich(es) in the basket and air-fry undisturbed for 8 minutes, or until browned and crunchy.
5. Use a nonstick-safe spatula, and perhaps a flatware fork for balance, to transfer the sandwich(es) to a cutting board. Cool for 2 or 3 minutes before slicing in half and serving.

Variations & Ingredients Tips:

- Substitute corned beef with pastrami for a classic New York deli taste.
- Use Thousand Island dressing instead of Russian dressing for a tangy, sweet flavor.
- Add sliced dill pickles or mustard to the sandwich for extra zing.

Per Serving (1 sandwich): Calories: 520; Cholesterol: 75mg; Total Fat: 30g; Saturated Fat: 9g; Sodium: 2020mg; Total Carbohydrates: 36g; Dietary Fiber: 4g; Total Sugars: 6g; Protein: 29g

Chicken Apple Brie Melt

Servings: 3 | Prep Time: 10 Minutes | Cooking Time: 13 Minutes

Ingredients:

- 3 140 to 170-gram boneless skinless chicken breasts
- Vegetable oil spray
- 1½ teaspoons Dried herbes de Provence
- 85 grams Brie, rind removed, thinly sliced
- 6 Thin cored apple slices
- 3 French rolls (gluten-free, if a concern)
- 2 tablespoons Dijon mustard (gluten-free, if a concern)

Directions:

1. Preheat the air fryer to 190°C/375°F.

2. Lightly coat all sides of the chicken breasts with vegetable oil spray. Sprinkle the breasts evenly with the herbes de Provence.
3. When the machine is at temperature, set the breasts in the basket and air-fry undisturbed for 10 minutes.
4. Top the chicken breasts with the apple slices, then the cheese. Air-fry undisturbed for 2 minutes, or until the cheese is melty and bubbling.
5. Use a nonstick-safe spatula and kitchen tongs, for balance, to transfer the breasts to a cutting board. Set the rolls in the basket and air-fry for 1 minute to warm through. (Putting them in the machine without splitting them keeps the insides very soft while the outside gets a little crunchy.)
6. Transfer the rolls to the cutting board. Split them open lengthwise, then spread 1 teaspoon mustard on each cut side. Set a prepared chicken breast on the bottom of a roll and close with its top, repeating as necessary to make additional sandwiches. Serve warm.

Variations & Ingredients Tips:

- Substitute the Brie with Camembert or another soft cheese of your choice.
- Use pears instead of apples for a different flavor profile.
- Add baby spinach or arugula for extra greens and nutrition.

Per Serving: Calories: 510; Cholesterol: 135mg; Total Fat: 19g; Saturated Fat: 8g; Sodium: 670mg; Total Carbohydrates: 41g; Dietary Fiber: 2g; Total Sugars: 6g; Protein: 45g

Best-ever Roast Beef Sandwiches

Servings: 6 | Prep Time: 10 Minutes | Cooking Time: 30-50 Minutes

Ingredients:

- 2½ teaspoons Olive oil
- 1½ teaspoons Dried oregano
- 1½ teaspoons Dried thyme
- 1½ teaspoons Onion powder
- 1½ teaspoons Table salt
- 1½ teaspoons Ground black pepper
- 1 kg Beef eye of round
- 6 Round soft rolls, such as Kaiser rolls or hamburger buns (gluten-free, if a concern), split open lengthwise
- ¾ cup Regular, low-fat, or fat-free mayonnaise (gluten-free, if a concern)
- 6 Romaine lettuce leaves, rinsed
- 6 Round tomato slices (0.5 cm thick)

Directions:

1. Preheat the air fryer to 180°C/350°F.
2. Mix the oil, oregano, thyme, onion powder, salt, and pepper in a small bowl. Spread this mixture all over the eye of round.
3. When the machine is at temperature, set the beef in the basket and air-fry for 30 to 50 minutes (the range depends on the size of the cut), turning the meat twice, until an instant-read meat thermometer inserted into the thickest piece of the meat registers 55°C/130°F for rare, 60°C/140°F for medium, or 65°C/150°F for well-done.
4. Use kitchen tongs to transfer the beef to a cutting board. Cool for 10 minutes. If serving now, carve into 3-mm-thick slices. Spread each roll with 2 tablespoons mayonnaise and divide the beef slices between the rolls. Top with a lettuce leaf and a tomato slice and serve. Or set the beef in a container, cover, and refrigerate for up to 3 days to make cold roast beef sandwiches anytime.

Variations & Ingredients Tips:

- Experiment with different herbs and spices in the rub, such as garlic powder, paprika, or rosemary.
- Add sliced red onions or pickles for extra flavor and crunch.
- Use leftover roast beef for cold sandwiches or salads.

Per Serving: Calories: 560; Cholesterol: 115mg; Total Fat: 27g; Saturated Fat: 6g; Sodium: 980mg; Total Carbohydrates: 32g; Dietary Fiber: 2g; Total Sugars: 4g; Protein: 47g

Perfect Burgers

Servings: 3 | Prep Time: 10 Minutes | Cooking Time: 13 Minutes

Ingredients:

- 510 grams 90% lean ground beef
- 1½ tablespoons Worcestershire sauce (gluten-free, if a concern)
- ½ teaspoon Ground black pepper
- 3 Hamburger buns (gluten-free if a concern), split open

Directions:

1. Preheat the air fryer to 190°C/375°F.
2. Gently mix the ground beef, Worcestershire sauce, and pepper in a bowl until well combined but preserving as much of the meat's fibers as possible. Divide this mixture into two 15-cm patties for the small batch, three 12.5-cm patties for the medium, or four 12.5-cm patties for the large. Make a thumbprint indentation in the center of each patty, about halfway through the meat.
3. Set the patties in the basket in one layer with some space between them. Air-fry undisturbed for 10 minutes, or until an instant-read meat thermometer inserted into the center of a burger registers 70°C/160°F (a medium-well burger). You may need to add 2 minutes cooking time if the air fryer is at 180°C/360°F.
4. Use a nonstick-safe spatula, and perhaps a flatware fork for balance, to transfer the burgers to a cutting board. Set the buns cut side down in the basket in one layer (working in batches as necessary) and air-fry undisturbed for 1 minute, to toast a bit and warm up. Serve the burgers in the warm buns.

Variations & Ingredients Tips:

- Mix in finely chopped onions, garlic, or herbs to the burger mixture for extra flavor.
- Use a mixture of ground beef and ground pork or lamb for a juicier, more flavorful burger.
- Top burgers with your favorite cheese, bacon, avocado, or sautéed mushrooms.

Per Serving (1 burger): Calories: 420; Cholesterol: 105mg; Total Fat: 22g; Saturated Fat: 8g; Sodium: 460mg; Total Carbohydrates: 23g; Dietary Fiber: 1g; Total Sugars: 3g; Protein: 34g

Philly Cheesesteak Sandwiches

Servings: 3 | Prep Time: 10 Minutes | Cooking Time: 9 Minutes

Ingredients:

- 340 grams Shaved beef
- 1 tablespoon Worcestershire sauce (gluten-free, if a concern)
- ¼ teaspoon Garlic powder
- ¼ teaspoon Mild paprika
- 6 tablespoons (45 grams) Frozen bell pepper strips (do not thaw)
- 2 slices, broken into rings Very thin yellow or white medium onion slice(s)
- 170 grams (6 to 8 slices) Provolone cheese slices
- 3 Long soft rolls such as hero, hoagie, or Italian sub rolls, or hot dog buns (gluten-free, if a concern), split open lengthwise

Directions:

1. Preheat the air fryer to 200°C/400°F.
2. When the machine is at temperature, spread the shaved beef in the basket, leaving a 1.25-cm perimeter around the meat for good air flow. Sprinkle the meat with the Worcestershire sauce, paprika, and garlic powder. Spread the peppers and onions on top of the meat.
3. Air-fry undisturbed for 6 minutes, or until cooked through. Set the cheese on top of the meat. Continue air-frying undisturbed for 3 minutes, or until the cheese has melted.
4. Use kitchen tongs to divide the meat and cheese layers in the basket between the rolls or buns. Serve hot.

Variations & Ingredients Tips:

- Use thinly sliced ribeye or sirloin steak instead of shaved beef for a more traditional texture.
- Add sliced mushrooms to the pepper and onion mixture for extra flavor and nutrition.
- Substitute provolone with American cheese or Cheez Whiz for a classic Philly taste.

Per Serving: Calories: 620; Cholesterol: 135mg; Total Fat: 32g; Saturated Fat: 15g; Sodium: 1320mg; Total Carbohydrates: 38g; Dietary Fiber: 2g; Total Sugars: 5g; Protein: 48g

Desserts And Sweets

Dark Chocolate Cream Galette

Servings: 4 | Prep Time: 15 Minutes | Cooking Time: 55 Minutes + Cooling Time

Ingredients:

- 454 grams cream cheese, softened
- 1 cup crumbled graham crackers
- 1 cup dark cocoa powder
- ½ cup white sugar
- 1 tsp peppermint extract
- 1 tsp ground cinnamon
- 1 egg
- 1 cup condensed milk
- 2 tbsp muscovado sugar
- 1 ½ tsp butter, melted

Directions:

1. Preheat air fryer to 180°C/350°F.
2. Place the crumbled graham crackers in a large bowl and stir in the muscovado sugar and melted butter. Spread the mixture into a greased pie pan, pressing down to form the galette base.
3. Place the pan into the air fryer and Bake for 5 minutes. Remove the pan and set aside.
4. Place the cocoa powder, cream cheese, peppermint extract, white sugar, cinnamon, condensed milk, and egg in a large bowl and whip thoroughly to combine.
5. Spoon the chocolate mixture over the graham cracker crust and level the top with a spatula. Put in the air fryer and Bake for 40 minutes until firm.
6. Transfer the galette to a wire rack to cool. Serve and enjoy!

Variations & Ingredients Tips:

- Use milk chocolate or white chocolate instead of dark for a sweeter flavor.
- Add espresso powder or instant coffee to the filling for a mocha twist.
- Top with fresh berries, whipped cream, or a dusting of powdered sugar.

Per Serving: Calories: 780; Total Fat: 50g; Saturated Fat: 29g; Sodium: 510mg; Total Carbohydrates: 77g; Dietary Fiber: 5g; Total Sugars: 61g; Protein: 15g

Blueberry Crisp

Servings: 6 | Prep Time: 10 Minutes | Cooking Time: 13 Minutes

Ingredients:

- 3 cups Fresh or thawed frozen blueberries
- 1/3 cup Granulated white sugar
- 1 tablespoon Instant tapioca
- 1/3 cup All-purpose flour
- 1/3 cup Rolled oats (not quick-cooking or steel-cut)
- 1/3 cup Chopped walnuts or pecans
- 1/3 cup Packed light brown sugar
- 5 tablespoons plus 1 teaspoon (2/3 stick) Butter, melted and cooled
- 3/4 teaspoon Ground cinnamon
- 1/4 teaspoon Table salt

Directions:

1. Preheat the air fryer to 200°C/400°F.
2. Mix the blueberries, granulated sugar, and instant tapioca in a 15cm, 18cm or 20cm round cake pan.
3. Set the pan in the basket and air-fry for 5 minutes, until blueberries begin to bubble.
4. Meanwhile, mix flour, oats, nuts, brown sugar, butter, cinnamon, and salt in a bowl.
5. When blueberries bubble, crumble flour mixture evenly on top.
6. Continue air-frying for 8 minutes until topping is browned and filling is bubbling.
7. Transfer pan to a wire rack and cool at least 10 minutes before serving.

Variations & Ingredients Tips:

- Use other berries like raspberries or blackberries.
- Add lemon or orange zest to the crisp topping.
- Serve warm with a scoop of vanilla ice cream.

Per Serving: Calories: 322; Total Fat: 15g; Saturated Fat: 6g; Sodium: 122mg; Total Carbohydrates: 45g; Dietary Fiber: 3g; Total Sugars: 25g; Protein: 4g

Spanish Churro Bites

Servings: 5 | Prep Time: 15 Minutes | Cooking Time: 35 Minutes

Ingredients:

- 1/4 tsp salt
- 2 tbsp vegetable oil
- 3 tbsp white sugar
- 1 cup flour
- 1/2 tsp ground cinnamon
- 2 tbsp granulated sugar

Directions:

1. On the stovetop, add 1 cup of water, salt, 1 tbsp of vegetable oil and 1 tbsp sugar in a pot. Bring to a boil over high heat.
2. Remove from the heat and add flour. Stir with a wooden spoon until the flour is combined and a ball of dough forms. Cool for 5 minutes.
3. Put the ball of dough in a plastic pastry bag with a star tip. Squeeze the dough to the tip and twist the top of the bag. Squeeze 10 strips of dough, about 13cm long each, onto a workspace. Spray with cooking oil.
4. Preheat air fryer to 170°C/340°F.
5. Place the churros in the greased frying basket and Air Fry for 22-25 minutes, flipping once halfway through until golden.
6. Meanwhile, heat the remaining vegetable oil in a small bowl. In another shallow bowl, mix the remaining 2 tbsp sugar and cinnamon.
7. Roll the cooked churros in cinnamon sugar. Top with granulated sugar and serve immediately.

Variations & Ingredients Tips:

▶ Serve with a thick hot chocolate or caramel dipping sauce.
▶ Add a teaspoon of vanilla extract to the dough.
▶ Stuff with chocolate or cream filling after baking.

Per Serving: Calories: 235; Total Fat: 6g; Saturated Fat: 1g; Cholesterol: 0mg; Sodium: 135mg; Total Carbs: 42g; Dietary Fiber: 1g; Total Sugars: 10g; Protein: 4g

Fruity Oatmeal Crisp

Servings: 6 | Prep Time: 15 Minutes | Cooking Time: 25 Minutes

Ingredients:

- 2 peeled nectarines, chopped
- 1 peeled apple, chopped
- 1/3 cup raisins
- 2 tbsp honey
- 1/3 cup brown sugar
- ¼ cup flour
- ½ cup oatmeal
- 3 tbsp softened butter

Directions:

1. Preheat air fryer to 190°C/380°F.
2. Mix together nectarines, apple, raisins, and honey in a baking pan. Set aside.
3. Mix brown sugar, flour, oatmeal and butter in a medium bowl until crumbly.
4. Top the fruit in a greased pan with the crumble.
5. Bake until bubbly and the topping is golden, 10-12 minutes.
6. Serve warm and top with vanilla ice cream if desired.

Variations & Ingredients Tips:

▶ Use different fruits like peaches, plums, berries, or pears.
▶ Substitute honey with maple syrup or agave nectar.
▶ Add chopped nuts like almonds, pecans, or walnuts to the crumble topping.

Per Serving: Calories: 250; Total Fat: 8g; Saturated Fat: 5g; Sodium: 65mg; Total Carbohydrates: 45g; Dietary Fiber: 3g; Total Sugars: 32g; Protein: 2g

Nutty Cookies

Servings: 6 | Prep Time: 10 Minutes | Cooking Time: 25 Minutes

Ingredients:

- 1/4 cup pistachios
- 1/4 cup evaporated cane sugar
- 1/4 cup raw almonds
- 1/2 cup almond flour
- 1 tsp pure vanilla extract
- 1 egg white

Directions:

1. Preheat air fryer to 190°C/375°F.
2. Add 1/4 cup of pistachios and almonds into a food processor. Pulse until they resemble crumbles.
3. Roughly chop the rest of the pistachios with a sharp knife.
4. Combine all ingredients in a large bowl until completely incorporated.
5. Form 6 equally-sized balls and transfer to the parchment-lined frying basket. Allow for 2.5-cm between each portion.
6. Bake for 7 minutes. Cool on a wire rack for 5 minutes. Serve and enjoy.

Variations & Ingredients Tips:

- Substitute other nuts like walnuts or pecans for some of the nuts.
- Add 1/4 cup dried fruit like cranberries or cherries.
- Drizzle with melted chocolate after cooling.

Per Serving: Calories: 190; Total Fat: 13g; Saturated Fat: 1g; Cholesterol: 0mg; Sodium: 25mg; Total Carbs: 14g; Dietary Fiber: 3g; Total Sugars: 8g; Protein: 6g

Cinnamon Canned Biscuit Donuts

Servings: 4 | Prep Time: 10 Minutes | Cooking Time: 25 Minutes

Ingredients:

- 1 can jumbo biscuits
- 1 cup cinnamon sugar

Directions:

1. Preheat air fryer to 180°C/360°F.
2. Separate biscuits into 8 pieces and cut a hole in the center of each.
3. Place 4 biscuit donuts in the air fryer basket. Spray with oil.
4. Bake for 8 minutes, flipping once halfway.
5. While still warm, coat donuts in cinnamon sugar mixture.
6. Serve immediately.

Variations & Ingredients Tips:

- Use a glaze or powdered sugar coating instead of cinnamon sugar.
- Fill the centers with fruit jam or chocolate hazelnut spread.
- Drizzle with melted butter before coating in cinnamon sugar.

Per Serving (2 donuts): Calories: 262; Total Fat: 6g; Saturated Fat: 1g; Sodium: 469mg; Total Carbohydrates: 51g; Dietary Fiber: 1g; Total Sugars: 24g; Protein: 4g

Orange Gooey Butter Cake

Servings: 6 | Prep Time: 30 Minutes | Cooking Time: 85 Minutes

Ingredients:

- Crust Layer:
- 1/2 cup flour
- 1/4 cup sugar
- 1/2 teaspoon baking powder
- 1/8 teaspoon salt
- 56-g (1/2 stick) unsalted European style butter, melted
- 1 egg
- 1 teaspoon orange extract
- 2 tablespoons orange zest
- Gooey Butter Layer:
- 226-g cream cheese, softened
- 113-g (1 stick) unsalted European style butter, melted
- 2 eggs
- 2 teaspoons orange extract
- 2 tablespoons orange zest
- 4 cups powdered sugar
- Garnish:
- Powdered sugar
- Orange slices

Directions:

1. Preheat the air fryer to 175°C/350°F.
2. Grease a 18-cm cake pan and line the bottom with parchment paper. Combine the flour, sugar, baking powder and salt in a bowl. Add the melted butter, egg, orange extract and orange zest. Mix well and press this mixture into the bottom of the greased cake pan. Lower the pan into the basket using an aluminum foil sling (fold a piece of aluminum foil into a strip about 5-cm wide by 60-cm long). Fold the ends of the aluminum foil over the top of the dish before returning the basket to the air fryer. Air-fry uncovered for 8 minutes.
3. To make the gooey butter layer, beat the cream cheese, melted butter, eggs, orange extract and orange zest in a large bowl using an electric hand mixer. Add the

powdered sugar in stages, beat until smooth with each addition. Pour this mixture on top of the baked crust in the cake pan. Wrap the pan with a piece of greased aluminum foil, tenting the top of the foil to leave a little room for the cake to rise.
4. Air-fry for 60 minutes at 175°C/350°F. Remove the aluminum foil and air-fry for an additional 17 minutes.
5. Let the cake cool inside the pan for at least 10 minutes. Then, run a butter knife around the cake and let the cake cool completely in the pan. When cooled, run the butter knife around the edges of the cake again and invert it onto a plate and then back onto a serving platter. Sprinkle the powdered sugar over the top of the cake and garnish with orange slices.

Variations & Ingredients Tips:

- Use Meyer lemons instead of oranges for a tart lemon flavor.
- Top with candied orange peel or drizzle with an orange glaze.
- Bake in ramekins for individual servings.

Per Serving: Calories: 730; Total Fat: 36g; Saturated Fat: 22g; Cholesterol: 175mg; Sodium: 280mg; Total Carbs: 101g; Dietary Fiber: 1g; Total Sugars: 86g; Protein: 7g

Cherry Hand Pies

Servings: 8 | Prep Time: 20 Minutes | Cooking Time: 8 Minutes

Ingredients:

- 4 cups frozen or canned pitted tart cherries (if using canned, drain and pat dry)
- 2 teaspoons lemon juice
- 1/2 cup sugar
- 1/4 cup cornstarch
- 1 teaspoon vanilla extract
- 1 Basic Pie Dough (see the preceding recipe) or store-bought pie dough

Directions:

1. In a saucepan, cook cherries and lemon juice over medium heat for 10 minutes until cherries break down.
2. Mix sugar and cornstarch, then stir into cherries. Cook 2-3 minutes until thickened.
3. Remove from heat, stir in vanilla and let cool to room temp (30 mins).
4. Divide pie dough into 8 pieces. Roll each into a circle 0.5-cm thick.
5. Place 1/4 cup filling in the center of each circle. Fold into a half-circle and crimp edges with a fork to seal. Prick tops.
6. Preheat air fryer to 175°C/350°F.
7. Place pies in single layer in air fryer basket and spray with cooking spray.
8. Cook for 8-10 minutes until golden brown.

Variations & Ingredients Tips:

- Use other fruit fillings like apple, blueberry or peach.
- Brush tops with egg wash before baking for a shiny finish.
- Dust with powdered sugar or drizzle with glaze after baking.

Per Serving: Calories: 267; Total Fat: 9g; Saturated Fat: 3g; Sodium: 116mg; Total Carbohydrates: 44g; Dietary Fiber: 2g; Total Sugars: 22g; Protein: 3g

Cheesecake Wontons

Servings: 16 | Prep Time: 20 Minutes | Cooking Time: 6 Minutes

Ingredients:

- 1/4 cup Regular or low-fat cream cheese (not fat-free)
- 2 tablespoons Granulated white sugar
- 1 1/2 tablespoons Egg yolk
- 1/4 teaspoon Vanilla extract
- 1/8 teaspoon Table salt
- 1 1/2 tablespoons All-purpose flour
- 16 Wonton wrappers (vegetarian, if a concern)
- Vegetable oil spray

Directions:

1. Preheat air fryer to 200°C/400°F.
2. Mash cream cheese, sugar, egg yolk, vanilla and salt until smooth.
3. Add flour and mash until fully combined.
4. Place 1 tsp filling in center of a wonton wrapper. Wet edges and fold into a triangle, sealing edges.
5. Fold side corners over filling and press to seal into a wonton shape.
6. Repeat with remaining wrappers and filling.
7. Mist wontons with oil spray on all sides.
8. Air fry for 6 minutes until golden brown and crisp.
9. Transfer to a wire rack and cool 5 minutes before serving.

Variations & Ingredients Tips:

▸ Add lemon or orange zest to the cheesecake filling.
▸ Brush with melted butter instead of oil spray.
▸ Serve with berry compote or chocolate sauce for dipping.

Per Serving (2 wontons): Calories: 66; Total Fat: 3g; Saturated Fat: 1g; Sodium: 65mg; Total Carbohydrates: 8g; Dietary Fiber: 0g; Total Sugars: 2g; Protein: 2g

Fruit Turnovers

Servings: 6 | Prep Time: 15 Minutes | Cooking Time: 25 Minutes

Ingredients:

- 1 sheet puff pastry dough
- 6 tsp peach preserves
- 3 kiwi, sliced
- 1 large egg, beaten
- 1 tbsp icing sugar

Directions: | Prepare puff pastry by cutting it into 6 rectangles. Roll out the pastry with a rolling pin into 13-cm squares. On your workspace, position one square so that it looks like a diamond with points to the top and bottom.

10. Spoon 1 tsp of the preserves on the bottom half and spread it, leaving a 1-cm border from the edge. Place half of one kiwi on top of the preserves. Brush the clean edges with the egg, then fold the top corner over the filling to make a triangle. Crimp with a fork to seal the pastry. Brush the top of the pastry with egg.
11. Preheat air fryer to 180°C/350°F.
12. Put the pastries in the greased air fryer basket. Air Fry for 10 minutes, flipping once until golden and puffy.
13. Remove from the fryer, let cool and dust with icing sugar. Serve.

Variations & Ingredients Tips:

▸ Use different fruit preserves like strawberry, raspberry, or apricot.
▸ Substitute kiwi with sliced peaches, plums, or pears.
▸ Add a sprinkle of cinnamon or nutmeg to the filling for extra flavor.

Per Serving: Calories: 240; Total Fat: 12g; Saturated Fat: 3g; Sodium: 95mg; Total Carbohydrates: 32g; Dietary Fiber: 2g; Total Sugars: 15g; Protein: 4g

Midnight Nutella® Banana Sandwich

Servings: 2 | Prep Time: 5 Minutes | Cooking Time: 8 Minutes

Ingredients:

- Butter, softened
- 4 slices white bread*
- 1/4 cup chocolate hazelnut spread (Nutella®)
- 1 banana

Directions:

1. Preheat air fryer to 190°C/370°F.
2. Butter one side of all bread slices.
3. Flip over and spread Nutella on the other sides.
4. Slice banana and place pieces on 2 bread slices. Top with remaining bread, buttered side up.
5. Cut sandwiches in half and place in air fryer basket.
6. Air fry for 5 minutes, then flip and cook 2-3 more minutes until browned.
7. Let cool slightly before serving.

Variations & Ingredients Tips:

▸ Use different nut butters like almond or cashew.
▸ Add sliced strawberries or marshmallow fluff.
▸ Use brioche, challah or other soft bread.

Per Serving (1 sandwich): Calories: 453; Total Fat: 21g; Saturated Fat: 7g; Sodium: 375mg; Total Carbohydrates: 59g; Dietary Fiber: 4g; Total Sugars: 24g; Protein: 9g

Giant Vegan Chocolate Chip Cookie

Servings: 4 | Prep Time: 15 Minutes | Cooking Time: 16 Minutes

Ingredients:

- ⅔ cup All-purpose flour
- 5 tablespoons Rolled oats (not quick-cooking or steel-cut oats)
- ¼ teaspoon Baking soda
- ¼ teaspoon Table salt
- 5 tablespoons Granulated white sugar
- ¼ cup Vegetable oil
- 2½ tablespoons Tahini
- 2½ tablespoons Maple syrup

- 2 teaspoons Vanilla extract
- ⅔ cup Vegan semisweet or bittersweet chocolate chips
- Baking spray

Directions:

1. Preheat the air fryer to 165°C/325°F (or 165°C/330°F, if that's the closest setting).
2. Whisk the flour, oats, baking soda, and salt in a bowl until well combined.
3. Using an electric hand mixer at medium speed, beat the sugar, oil, tahini, maple syrup, and vanilla until rich and creamy, about 3 minutes, scraping down the inside of the bowl occasionally.
4. Scrape down and remove the beaters. Fold in the flour mixture and chocolate chips with a rubber spatula just until all the flour is moistened and the chocolate chips are even throughout the dough.
5. For a small air fryer, coat the inside of a 15-cm round cake pan with baking spray. For a medium air fryer, coat the inside of an 18-cm round cake pan with baking spray. And for a large air fryer, coat the inside of a 20-cm round cake pan with baking spray. Scrape and gently press the dough into the prepared pan, spreading it into an even layer to the perimeter.
6. Set the pan in the basket and air-fry undisturbed for 16 minutes, or until puffed, browned, and firm to the touch.
7. Transfer the pan to a wire rack and cool for 10 minutes. Loosen the cookie from the perimeter with a spatula, then invert the pan onto a cutting board and let the cookie come free. Remove the pan and reinvert the cookie onto the wire rack. Cool for 5 minutes more before slicing into wedges to serve.

Variations & Ingredients Tips:

- Use almond butter or sunflower seed butter instead of tahini.
- Add chopped nuts like walnuts or pecans to the dough.
- Sprinkle with flaky sea salt before baking for a sweet-salty contrast.

Per Serving: Calories: 490; Total Fat: 28g; Saturated Fat: 6g; Sodium: 210mg; Total Carbohydrates: 60g; Dietary Fiber: 4g; Total Sugars: 34g; Protein: 6g

Donut Holes

Servings: 13 | Prep Time: 15 Minutes | Cooking Time: 12 Minutes

Ingredients:

- 6 tablespoons Granulated white sugar
- 1½ tablespoons Butter, melted and cooled
- 2 tablespoons (or 1 small egg, well beaten) Pasteurized egg substitute, such as Egg Beaters
- 6 tablespoons Regular or low-fat sour cream (not fat-free)
- ¾ teaspoon Vanilla extract
- 1⅔ cups All-purpose flour
- ¾ teaspoon Baking powder
- ¼ teaspoon Table salt
- Vegetable oil spray

Directions:

1. Preheat the air fryer to 180°C/350°F.
2. Whisk the sugar and melted butter in a medium bowl until well combined. Whisk in the egg substitute or egg, then the sour cream and vanilla until smooth. Remove the whisk and stir in the flour, baking powder, and salt with a wooden spoon just until a soft dough forms.
3. Use 2 tablespoons of this dough to create a ball between your clean palms. Set it aside and continue making balls: 8 more for the small batch, 12 more for the medium batch, or 17 more for the large one.
4. Coat the balls in the vegetable oil spray, then set them in the basket with as much air space between them as possible. Even a fraction of 0.25 cm will be enough, but they should not touch. Air-fry undisturbed for 12 minutes, or until browned and cooked through. A toothpick inserted into the center of a ball should come out clean.
5. Pour the contents of the basket onto a wire rack. Cool for at least 5 minutes before serving.

Variations & Ingredients Tips:

- Toss the warm donut holes in cinnamon sugar or powdered sugar.
- Add grated lemon or orange zest to the batter for a citrusy flavor.
- Fill the donut holes with jam, Nutella, or pastry cream using a piping bag.

Per Serving: Calories: 130; Total Fat: 5g; Saturated Fat: 3g; Sodium: 100mg; Total Carbohydrates: 20g; Dietary Fiber: 0g; Total Sugars: 9g; Protein: 2g

S'mores Pockets

Servings: 6 | Prep Time: 15 Minutes | Cooking

Time: 5 Minutes

Ingredients:

- 12 sheets phyllo dough, thawed
- 1 1/2 cups butter, melted
- 3/4 cup graham cracker crumbs
- 1 (200g) Giant Hershey's® milk chocolate bar
- 12 marshmallows, cut in half

Directions:

1. Place one sheet of the phyllo on a large cutting board. Keep the rest of the phyllo sheets covered with a slightly damp, clean kitchen towel. Brush the phyllo sheet generously with some melted butter. Place a second phyllo sheet on top of the first and brush it with more butter. Repeat with one more phyllo sheet until you have a stack of 3 phyllo sheets with butter brushed between the layers.
2. Cover the phyllo sheets with one quarter of the graham cracker crumbs leaving a 5cm border on one of the short ends of the rectangle. Cut the phyllo sheets lengthwise into 3 strips.
3. Take 2 of the strips and crisscross them to form a cross with the empty borders at the top and to the left. Place 2 of the chocolate rectangles in the center of the cross. Place 4 of the marshmallow halves on top of the chocolate.
4. Now fold the pocket together by folding the bottom phyllo strip up over the chocolate and marshmallows. Then fold the right side over, then the top strip down and finally the left side over. Brush all the edges generously with melted butter to seal shut.
5. Repeat with the next three sheets of phyllo, until all the sheets have been used. You will be able to make 2 pockets with every second batch because you will have an extra graham cracker crumb strip from the previous set of sheets.
6. Preheat the air fryer to 175°C/350°F.
7. Transfer 3 pockets at a time to the air fryer basket. Air-fry at 175°C/350°F for 4 to 5 minutes, until the phyllo dough is light brown in color. Flip the pockets over halfway through the cooking process. Repeat with the remaining 3 pockets.
8. Serve warm.

Variations & Ingredients Tips:

- Use different chocolate bar flavors like dark chocolate or peanut butter cups.
- Substitute marshmallows with marshmallow fluff or creme.
- Sprinkle crushed graham crackers on top before serving.

Per Serving: Calories: 625; Total Fat: 41g; Saturated Fat: 24g; Cholesterol: 95mg; Sodium: 590mg; Total Carbs: 55g; Dietary Fiber: 2g; Total Sugars: 16g; Protein: 7g

Guilty Chocolate Cookies

Servings: 6 | Prep Time: 10 Minutes | Cooking Time: 25 Minutes

Ingredients:

- 3 eggs, beaten
- 1 tsp vanilla extract
- 1 tsp apple cider vinegar
- 1/3 cup butter, softened
- 1/3 cup sugar
- ¼ cup cacao powder
- ¼ tsp baking soda

Directions:

1. Preheat air fryer to 150°C/300°F.
2. Combine eggs, vanilla extract, and apple vinegar in a bowl until well combined. Refrigerate for 5 minutes.
3. Whisk in butter and sugar until smooth, finally toss in cacao powder and baking soda until smooth.
4. Make balls out of the mixture. Place the balls onto the parchment-lined air fryer basket.
5. Bake for 13 minutes until brown.
6. Using a fork, flatten each cookie. Let cool completely before serving.

Variations & Ingredients Tips:

- Add chocolate chips, chopped nuts, or dried fruit to the dough for extra texture.
- Use coconut sugar or maple syrup instead of regular sugar for a healthier option.
- Serve with a glass of cold milk or a scoop of vanilla ice cream.

Per Serving: Calories: 220; Total Fat: 14g; Saturated Fat: 8g; Sodium: 140mg; Total Carbohydrates: 20g; Dietary Fiber: 2g; Total Sugars: 15g; Protein: 5g

Carrot-oat Cake Muffins

Servings: 4 | Prep Time: 10 Minutes | Cooking Time: 20 Minutes

Ingredients:

- 3 tbsp butter, softened
- ¼ cup brown sugar
- 1 tbsp maple syrup
- 1 egg white
- ½ tsp vanilla extract
- 1/3 cup finely grated carrots
- ½ cup oatmeal
- 1/3 cup flour
- ½ tsp baking soda
- ¼ cup raisins

Directions:

1. Preheat air fryer to 180°C/350°F.
2. Mix the butter, brown sugar, and maple syrup until smooth, then toss in the egg white, vanilla, and carrots. Whisk well and add the oatmeal, flour, baking soda, and raisins.
3. Divide the mixture between muffin cups.
4. Bake in the air fryer for 8-10 minutes.

Variations & Ingredients Tips:

- Use grated zucchini or apple instead of carrots.
- Substitute raisins with dried cranberries, chopped dates, or chocolate chips.
- Top with cream cheese frosting or a sprinkle of powdered sugar.

Per Serving: Calories: 250; Total Fat: 11g; Saturated Fat: 6g; Sodium: 230mg; Total Carbohydrates: 36g; Dietary Fiber: 2g; Total Sugars: 20g; Protein: 4g

Custard

Servings: 4 | Prep Time: 5 Minutes | Cooking Time: 45 Minutes

Ingredients:

- 2 cups whole milk
- 2 eggs
- ¼ cup sugar
- ⅛ teaspoon salt
- ¼ teaspoon vanilla
- cooking spray
- ⅛ teaspoon nutmeg

Directions:

1. In a blender, process milk, egg, sugar, salt, and vanilla until smooth.
2. Spray a 15x15-cm baking pan with nonstick spray and pour the custard into it.
3. Cook at 150°C/300°F for 45 minutes. Custard is done when the center sets.
4. Sprinkle top with the nutmeg.
5. Allow custard to cool slightly.
6. Serve it warm, at room temperature, or chilled.

Variations & Ingredients Tips:

- Infuse the milk with vanilla bean, cinnamon stick, or citrus zest for extra flavor.
- Use coconut milk or almond milk for a dairy-free version.
- Top with fresh fruit, caramel sauce, or chocolate shavings.

Per Serving: Calories: 170; Total Fat: 6g; Saturated Fat: 3g; Sodium: 160mg; Total Carbohydrates: 22g; Dietary Fiber: 0g; Total Sugars: 21g; Protein: 7g

Chocolate Soufflés

Servings: 2 | Prep Time: 15 Minutes | Cooking Time: 14 Minutes

Ingredients:

- Butter and sugar for greasing the ramekins
- 85-g semi-sweet chocolate, chopped
- 1/4 cup unsalted butter
- 2 eggs, yolks and whites separated
- 3 tablespoons sugar
- 1/2 teaspoon pure vanilla extract
- 2 tablespoons all-purpose flour
- Powdered sugar, for dusting
- Heavy cream, for serving

Directions:

1. Butter and sugar two 170-g ramekins.
2. Melt chocolate and butter together.
3. Beat egg yolks, then add sugar, vanilla and melted chocolate. Stir in flour.
4. Preheat air fryer to 165°C/330°F.
5. Whip egg whites to soft peaks, then fold into chocolate mixture.
6. Transfer batter to ramekins, leaving 1.3-cm at top.
7. Air fry for 14 minutes until risen and browned on top.
8. Dust with powdered sugar and serve immediately with cream.

Variations & Ingredients Tips:

- Add a splash of liqueur to the batter.
- Top with fresh berries before serving.

- Use ramekins with straight sides for better rise.

Per Serving: Calories: 575; Total Fat: 41g; Saturated Fat: 24g; Sodium: 165mg; Total Carbohydrates: 48g; Dietary Fiber: 3g; Total Sugars: 36g; Protein: 9g

Chocolate Macaroons

Servings: 16 | Prep Time: 15 Minutes | Cooking Time: 8 Minutes

Ingredients:

- 2 Large egg whites, at room temperature
- 1/8 teaspoon Table salt
- 1/2 cup Granulated white sugar
- 1 1/2 cups Unsweetened shredded coconut
- 3 tablespoons Unsweetened cocoa powder

Directions:

1. Preheat the air fryer to 190°C/375°F.
2. Beat the egg whites and salt until stiff peaks form.
3. Gradually beat in the sugar until meringue is shiny and thick.
4. Fold in the coconut and cocoa gently until combined.
5. Scoop 2 tbsp portions and roll into balls (16 total).
6. Line air fryer basket with parchment paper and place balls with space between.
7. Air fry for 8 minutes until dry and lightly browned.
8. Transfer to a wire rack and cool at least 10 minutes before serving.

Variations & Ingredients Tips:

- Use sweetened shredded coconut for a sweeter macaroon.
- Add a teaspoon of instant coffee or espresso powder to the cocoa.
- Drizzle with melted chocolate after baking.

Per Serving (1 macaroon): Calories: 72; Total Fat: 3g; Saturated Fat: 2g; Sodium: 34mg; Total Carbohydrates: 11g; Dietary Fiber: 1g; Total Sugars: 9g; Protein: 1g

Peanut Butter S'mores

Servings: 10 | Prep Time: 10 Minutes | Cooking Time: 1 Minute

Ingredients:

- 10 Graham crackers (full, double-square cookies as they come out of the package)
- 5 tablespoons natural-style creamy or crunchy peanut butter
- 1/2 cup milk chocolate chips
- 10 standard-size marshmallows (not minis and not jumbo campfire ones)

Directions:

1. Preheat the air fryer to 175°C/350°F.
2. Break the graham crackers in half widthwise at the marked place, so the rectangle is now in two squares. Set half of the squares flat side up on your work surface. Spread each with about 1 1/2 teaspoons peanut butter, then set 10 to 12 chocolate chips point side up into the peanut butter on each, pressing gently so the chips stick.
3. Flatten a marshmallow between your clean, dry hands and set it atop the chips. Do the same with the remaining marshmallows on the other coated graham crackers. Do not set the other half of the graham crackers on top of these coated graham crackers.
4. When the machine is at temperature, set the treats graham cracker side down in a single layer in the basket. They may touch, but even a fraction of an cm between them will provide better air flow. Air-fry undisturbed for 45 seconds.
5. Use a nonstick-safe spatula to transfer the topped graham crackers to a wire rack. Set the other graham cracker squares flat side down over the marshmallows. Cool for a couple of minutes before serving.

Variations & Ingredients Tips:

- Substitute peanut butter with almond butter, cashew butter or Nutella.
- Use dark chocolate chips or a mix of milk and dark for a richer flavor.
- Sprinkle a pinch of sea salt on top of the peanut butter for a sweet and salty twist.

Per Serving: Calories: 150; Total Fat: 7g; Saturated Fat: 2g; Cholesterol: 0mg; Sodium: 115mg; Total Carbs: 20g; Dietary Fiber: 1g; Total Sugars: 11g; Protein: 3g

INDEX

A

Apple Cornbread Stuffed Pork Loin With Apple Gravy	45
Apple-cinnamon-walnut Muffins	21
Aromatic Ahi Tuna Steaks	52
Asian Glazed Meatballs	77
Asy Carnitas	42

B

Baked Eggs	16
Banana-strawberry Cakecups	16
Basic Chicken Breasts	37
Basil Feta Crostini	26
Basil Mushroom & Shrimp Spaghetti	53
Beef & Barley Stuffed Bell Peppers	47
Beef & Spinach Sautée	48
Beef Fajitas	40
Beef Meatballs With Herbs	42
Beer-battered Cod	50
Beer-battered Onion Rings	26
Beet Fries	71
Best-ever Roast Beef Sandwiches	84
Better Fish Sticks	50
Black Bean Veggie Burgers	76
Blistered Green Beans	67
Blueberry Crisp	86
Breakfast Frittata	18
Buttered Brussels Sprouts	71

C

Caribbean Jerk Cod Fillets	51
Carrot-oat Cake Muffins	92
Cauliflower Steaks Gratin	59
Cheesecake Wontons	89
Cheesy Chicken-avocado Paninis	36
Cheesy Olive And Roasted Pepper Bread	16
Cheesy Pigs In A Blanket	22
Cherry Chipotle Bbq Chicken Wings	25
Cherry Hand Pies	89
Chicken Apple Brie Melt	83
Chicken Club Sandwiches	78
Chicken Hand Pies	34
Chicken Nuggets	36
Chicken Saltimbocca Sandwiches	75

Chicken Spiedies	79	Crunchy Clam Strips	53
Chicken Tenders With Basil-strawberry Glaze	36	Crunchy Falafel Balls	80
Chicken Wings Al Ajillo	39	Curried Cauliflower With Cashews And Yogurt	69
Chili Cheese Dogs	82	Custard	93
Chinese Firecracker Shrimp	57	**D**	
Chocolate Almond Crescent Rolls	13	Dark Chocolate Cream Galette	86
Chocolate Macaroons	94	Dijon Thyme Burgers	81
Chocolate Soufflés	93	Donut Holes	91
Christmas Chicken & Roasted Grape Salad	38	**E**	
Cilantro Sea Bass	54	Easy Cheese & Spinach Lasagna	62
Cinnamon Canned Biscuit Donuts	88	Easy Vanilla Muffins	19
Cinnamon Pita Chips	24	Easy Zucchini Lasagna Roll-ups	64
Cinnamon Pumpkin Donuts	17	Egg Muffins	21
Classic Crab Cakes	55	Egg Rolls	61
Coconut Curry Chicken With Coconut Rice	33	Eggplant Parmesan	64
Colorful Vegetable Medley	60	Eggplant Parmesan Subs	82
Cornish Hens With Honey-lime Glaze	38	**F**	
Crab Cakes	54	Famous Potato Au Gratin	71
Crab Toasts	24	Farfalle With White Sauce	60
Crispy Apple Fries With Caramel Sauce	65	Farmers Market Quiche	15
Crispy Chicken Cakes	20	Fiery Chicken Meatballs	38
Crispy Duck With Cherry Sauce	32	Filled French Toast	14
Crispy Lamb Shoulder Chops	46	Fish Cakes	51
		Fish Goujons With Tartar Sauce	57

Fish Sticks With Tartar Sauce	50
Fish Tortillas With Coleslaw	53
Flounder Fillets	56
Fried Corn On The Cob	73
Fried Goat Cheese	27
Fried Scallops	56
Fruit Turnovers	90
Fruity Oatmeal Crisp	87

G

Garlicky Brussels Sprouts	68
Giant Vegan Chocolate Chip Cookie	90
Gluten-free Nutty Chicken Fingers	39
Goat Cheese Stuffed Portobellos	66
Greek Pita Pockets	40
Greek-style Pork Stuffed Jalapeño Poppers	49
Guilty Chocolate Cookies	92

H

Halibut With Coleslaw	55
Hasselback Garlic-and-butter Potatoes	67
Hawaiian Chicken	33
Herbed Baby Red Potato Hasselback	73
Home-style Pumpkin Crumble	18
Honey Pork Links	41

I

Indian Fry Bread Tacos	47
Inside Out Cheeseburgers	81
Inside-out Cheeseburgers	75
Italian-style Fried Cauliflower	61

J

Jalapeño & Mozzarella Stuffed Mushrooms	29

K

Kale & Lentils With Crispy Onions	63
Kentucky-style Pork Tenderloin	42

L

Lamb Chops	44
Latkes	69
Lemon Sage Roast Chicken	31
Lobster Tails With Lemon Garlic Butter	49

M

Maple Loaded Sweet Potatoes	23
Mashed Potato Pancakes	68
Midnight Nutella® Banana Sandwich	90
Mini Everything Bagels	20
Moroccan-spiced Carrots	68
Mouth-watering Vegetable Casserole	28
Mustard And Rosemary Pork Tenderloin With Fried Apples	48

N

Nacho Chicken Fries	34
Nutty Cookies	87

O

Orange Gooey Butter Cake	88

P

Parmesan Asparagus	74
Peach Fritters	13
Peanut Butter S'mores	94
Perfect Burgers	84
Philly Cheesesteak Sandwiches	85
Philly Chicken Cheesesteak Stromboli	31
Pineapple & Veggie Souvlaki	59
Potato Samosas	30

Q

Quick Tuna Tacos	55

R

Rainbow Quinoa Patties	58
Reuben Sandwiches	83
Rich Clam Spread	22
Roast Sweet Potatoes With Parmesan	70
Roasted Garlic And Thyme Tomatoes	74
Roasted Tomatillo Salsa	26

S

S'mores Pockets	91
Sage Pork With Potatoes	44
Salmon Burgers	80
Saucy Chicken Thighs	37
Sausage & Cauliflower Balls	28
Sausage And Pepper Heros	79
Shrimp Toasts	25
Simple Roasted Sweet Potatoes	72
Simple Salsa Chicken Thighs	35
Smoked Paprika Cod Goujons	52
Smoky Sweet Potato Fries	66
Smooth Walnut-banana Loaf	14
Soft Pretzels	15
Spanish Churro Bites	87
Spiced Parsnip Chips	23
Spicy Bean Patties	62
Spicy Sweet Potato Tater-tots	23
Spinach-bacon Rollups	17
Steak Fingers	43
Stuffed Onions	70
Stuffed Portobellos	61
Stunning Apples & Onions	73
Sweet Corn Bread	59
Sweet Nutty Chicken Breasts	33
Sweet Potato Chips	29
Sweet-hot Pepperoni Pizza	19

T

T-bone Steak With Roasted Tomato, Corn And Asparagus Salsa 43

Taco Pie With Meatballs	45
Thai-style Crab Wontons	27
Thai-style Pork Sliders	78
Thanksgiving Turkey Sandwiches	76
Thyme Sweet Potato Chips	29
Thyme Sweet Potato Wedges	72
Tortilla Pizza Margherita	65
Tropical Salsa	58
Turkey-hummus Wraps	35
Tuscan Veal Chops	41

V

Vegetable Couscous	65
Vietnamese Gingered Tofu	63

W

Walnut Pancake	18
Wiener Schnitzel	46

Printed in Great Britain
by Amazon